D1769013

OFF THE GROUND

AN ANTHOLOGY OF POETRY

Compiled by

ALEXANDER HADDOW, B.A.

LATE

PRINCIPAL MASTER OF METHOD, THE TRAINING COLLEGE, GLASGOW

*Author of " On the Teaching of Poetry " and " The Ring and the
Book as a Connected Narrative"*

and

WILLIAM KERR, M.A.

LATE

DIRECTOR OF STUDIES, THE TRAINING COLLEGE, GLASGOW

Author of " The English Apprentice "

BOOK IV

Granger Index Reprint Series

BOOKS FOR LIBRARIES PRESS

FREEPORT, NEW YORK

STANDARD BOOK NUMBER:
8369-6067-X

LIBRARY OF CONGRESS CATALOG CARD NUMBER:
76-75516

ACKNOWLEDGMENTS

We value highly the permission to include copyright material in this anthology, and are happy to put on record our indebtedness for :

" THE FOX'S SKIN " to Miss Marion Angus and Messrs. Faber & Faber, Ltd.

" THE BUZZARDS " to Mr. Martin Armstrong.

" THE HAWK " to Mr. A. C. Benson and Messrs. John Lane, the Bodley Head, Ltd.

" THE DOWNS " to the Clarendon Press, publishers of " The Shorter Poems of Robert Bridges, 1931 ".

" EGYPT'S MIGHT IS TUMBLED DOWN " to Sir Henry Newbolt and Messrs. Elkin Mathews & Marrot, Ltd., publishers of " Poems by Mary E. Coleridge ".

" THE COMMON STREET " to Messrs. J. M. Dent, publishers of " A Chant of Love for England " by Helen Gray Cone.

" THE KINGFISHER " to Mr. W. H. Davies and Messrs. Jonathan Cape, Ltd., publishers of " Collected Poems of W. H. Davies ".

" A SONG OF SOLDIERS " and " JENNY WREN " to Mr. Walter de la Mare.

" WHEN THE TRAVELLER RETURNS " to Professor W. Macneile Dixon and Messrs. Blackie & Son, Ltd.

" THE TOLL-GATE HOUSE " to Messrs. Sidgwick & Jackson, publishers of " Collected Poems by John Drinkwater ".

" WAR SONG OF THE SARACENS " and " A SHIP, AN ISLE, A SICKLE MOON ", to Messrs. Martin Secker & Warburg, Ltd., publishers of " Collected Poems of James Elroy Flecker ".

" THE ICE CART " and " FLANNAN ISLE " to Mr. W. W. Gibson and Messrs. Macmillan & Co., Ltd., publishers of " Collected Poems 1905-1925 ".

" ENGLAND, MY ENGLAND " to the Author's Executors and Messrs Macmillan & Co., publishers of " The Poems of W. E. Henley ".

" THE HOWE O' THE MEARNS " to Mr. John Murray, publisher of " Songs of Angus " by Miss Violet Jacob.

" THE WAY THROUGH THE WOODS " to Mrs. Kipling and Messrs. Macmillan & Co., Ltd., publishers of " Rewards and Fairies ".

" THE BALLAD OF EAST AND WEST " to Mrs. Kipling and Messrs. Methuen & Co., publishers of " Barrack-Room Ballads ".

" FOR TO ADMIRE " to Mrs. Kipling and Messrs. Methuen & Co., publishers of " The Seven Seas ".

' THE RIDER AT THE GATE ", " TO-MORROW ", " ROADWAYS ", " THE DEAD KNIGHT ", reprinted from " Collected Poems of John Masefield " (Wm. Heinemann, Ltd.), by permission of the author.

"ADMIRAL DEATH", "THE GAY GORDONS", and "HE FELL AMONG THIEVES", to Sir Henry Newbolt and Mr. John Murray, publisher of "Poems New and Old".

"OLD GREY SQUIRREL", "THE MOON IS UP", and "SHERWOOD", to Mr. Alfred Noyes and Messrs. Wm. Blackwood & Sons, Ltd., publishers of "Collected Poems".

"ON A ROMAN HELMET" to Mr. W. H. Ogilvie.

"THE LARK'S SONG" (from "IN MERCER STREET") to Mr. Seumas O'Sullivan.

"KIRKBRIDE" to Messrs. Alexander Gardner, Ltd.

"EVERYONE SANG" to Mr. Siegfried Sassoon and Messrs. Wm. Heinemann, Ltd.

"THE GOAT PATHS" to Mr. James Stephens and Messrs. Macmillan & Co., Ltd., publishers of "Collected Poems".

"REQUIEM", "THE COUNTRY OF THE CAMISARDS", "THE HOUSE BEAUTIFUL", "TO S. R. CROCKETT", and "IN THE HIGHLANDS, IN THE COUNTRY PLACES", to Messrs. Chatto & Windus.

"SERENA SINGS" to Miss Jan Struther, and the proprietors of "Punch".

"THE FISH HAWK" to Mr. John H. Wheelock and Messrs. Charles Scribner's Sons, Ltd., publishers of "The Black Panther".

"THE QUEEN OF LOCHLIN" to Mr. John Grant, publisher of "Ossian and Macpherson, edited by William Sharp."

EXTRACT FROM "LEAVES FROM A VICEROY'S NOTEBOOK" by Lord Curzon, to Messrs. Macmillan & Co

CONTENTS

POEMS WITH QUESTIONS AND COMMENTS

CONTENTS—*Continued*

INDEX OF AUTHORS

Consider it warely, read oftor than anis,
Weill, at ane blenk, slee poetry nocht ta'en is.

GAVIN DOUGLAS
(1475-1522)

Dionysius Thrax gives **us** the definition ; a skill produced by practice, in the things said in poets and prose writers ; and he goes on to divide it into its six parts, of which the first and most essential is Reading Aloud. . . .

The Scholar's special duty is to turn the written signs in which old poetry or philosophy is now enshrined back into living thought or feeling. He must so understand as to re-live.

GILBERT MURRAY
(*Religio Grammatici*)

" For God's sake disagree with me," cried Cicero's young friend to the obsequious country-cousin at lunch with him, " so that there can be two of us." So now, if the reader does not agree with me about Romanticism, still he may find how to agree better with himself. For no one discovers what he really thinks, till he has crossed thoughts with others.

F. L. LUCAS
(*The Decline and Fall of the Romantic Ideal*)

OFF THE GROUND

PRACTICE IN RHYTHM

Not poetry nor the dance created rhythm; rather the instinct for rhythm created them.

J. A. K. THOMSON
(*Springs of Poetry*)

Metre, without doubt, is one of the most important things in poetry. Its importance is obvious in the instinctive pleasure we take in it; but the more finely we attend to the way it pleases us, the more pleasure shall we find it has to give us.

LASCELLES ABERCROMBIE
(*Poetry : Its Music and Meaning*)

Read the following extracts aloud:

I

For the Angel of Death spread his wings on the blast.
And breathed in the face of the foe as he passed;
And the eyes of the sleepers waxed deadly and chill,
And their hearts but once heaved, and for ever grew
    still.

BYRON
(**The Destruction of Sennacherib**)

II

Did you hear of the curate who mounted his mare,
And merrily trotted along to the fair?
Of creature more tractable none ever heard,
In the height of her speed she would stop at a word;
But again with a word, when the curate said, " Hey ! "
She put forth her mettle and galloped away.

PEACOCK
(**The Priest and the Mulberry Tree**)

13

III

I sprang to the stirrup, and Joris, and he ;
I galloped, Dirck galloped, we galloped all three ;
" Good speed ! " cried the watch, as the gate-bolts
    undrew ;
" Speed ! " echoed the wall to us galloping through ;
Behind shut the postern, the lights sank to rest,
And into the midnight we galloped abreast.

BROWNING
(*How They Brought the Good News from Ghent to Aix*)

1. Which of those stanzas do you read at the greatest speed, and which most slowly ?

2. As you see, they have all the same metre, *i.e.* the same number of strong accents, separated by the same number of weak accents, with the same occasional variation, one weak accent instead of two. Why then do we read one faster than another ?

3. The following passages are given to illustrate further this variation of pace. You should have no difficulty in deciding which of each couple goes the faster, and why. Why do you think I have added passage VII ?

Notes: page 209.

IV (1)

Come as the winds come, when
    Forests are rended.
Come as the waves come, when
    Navies are stranded.

SCOTT
(*Pibroch of Donuil Dhu*)

IV (2)

Take her up tenderly,
    Lift her with care ;
Fashioned so slenderly,
    Young and so fair.

HOOD
(*The Bridge of Sighs*)

*   *   *   *

V (1)

Haste thee, Nymph, and bring with thee
Jest and youthful Jollity, . . .
Sport that wrinkled Care derides,
And Laughter holding both his sides.
Come, and trip it as ye go
On the light fantastic toe.

MILTON
(*L'Allegro*)

V (2)

Come, pensive Nun, devout and pure,
Sober, steadfast, and demure,
All in a robe of darkest grain,
Flowing with majestic train . . .
Come, but keep thy wonted state,
With even step, and musing gait.

MILTON
(*Il Penseroso*)

* * * *

VI (1)

William, my teacher, my friend ! dear William and
    dear Dorothea !
Smooth out the folds of my letter, and place it on desk
    or on table ;
Place it on table or desk ; and your right hands
    loosely half-closing,
Gently sustain them in air, and extending the digit
    didactic,
Rest it a moment on each of the forks of the five-
    forkéd left hand,
Twice on the breadth of the thumb, and once on
    the tip of each finger ;
Read with a nod of the head in a humouring
    recitativo ;
And, as I live, you will see my hexameters hopping
    before you.
This is a galloping measure ; a hop, and a trot, and a
    gallop !

COLERIDGE
(*Hexameters*)

VI (2)

This is the forest primeval. The murmuring pines
    and the hemlocks,
Bearded with moss, and in garments green, indistinct
    in the twilight,
Stand like Druids of old, with voices sad and prophetic,
Stand like harpers hoar, with beards that rest on their
    bosoms.
Loud from its rocky caverns, the deep voiced
    neighbouring ocean
Speaks, and in accents disconsolate answers the wail of
    the forest.

LONGFELLOW
(*Evangeline*)

*   *   *   *

VII

There was a young bard of Japan,
Who wrote verses that no one could scan.
    They told him 'twas so :
    He replied, " Yes, I know,
But I always try to get as many words into the last
    line as I possibly can."

ANONYMOUS
(*From "The Comic Muse "*)

4. What, then, is the one important thing we have discovered
about rhythm ?

5. The most important thing to know about rhythm,
however, is contained in the quotations from Professor
Thomson and Professor Abercrombie, at the top of page
13. They use practically the same word to express it.
Can you find it ?

Notes : page 210.

18

PRACTICE IN RHYME

Read the following extract aloud :

I

Here are cool mosses deep,
And thro' the moss the ivies creep,
And in the stream the long-leaved flowers weep,
And from the craggy ledge the poppy hangs in sleep.

TENNYSON
(*The Lotos-Eaters*)

I

1. Where in the line do we look for the rhyme ?

2. The rhyme comes generally in the same place in the line.
   What effect does this produce?

3. Suppose passage I went thus :

   > *Here are cool mosses deep,*
   > *And here the ivies creep,*
   > *And the long-leaved flowers weep,*
   > *And the poppy hangs in sleep.*

   Though we have changed the rhythm and dropped some of
   the words, the rhyme scheme is still the same.   Why does
   it not produce the same effect ?

4. Suppose passage I went thus :

   > *Here are cool mosses soft,*
   > *And thro' the moss the ivies twist,*
   > *And in the stream the long-leaved flowers stand,*
   > *And from the craggy ledge the poppy hangs in sleep.*

   We have changed only the rhyme scheme.   The rhythm
   is exactly as it was, yet it does not produce the same
   effect.   Why ?

5. Which of the versions given in questions 3 and 4 do you
   prefer ?

Notes : page 211.

17

Read the following extract aloud :

II

I have lived long enough, having seen one thing, that
    love hath an end ;
Goddess and maiden and queen, be near me now and
    befriend.
Thou art more than the day or the morrow, the seasons
    that laugh or that weep ;
For these give joy and sorrow ; but thou, Proserpina,
    sleep.

SWINBURNE
(Hymn to Proserpine)

II

1. Draw up the rhyme scheme for passage II.

2. Suppose passage II went thus :

> *I have lived long enough, having found one thing, that love
>   hath an end ;*
> *Goddess and maiden and queen, be near me now and
>   befriend.*
> *Thou art more than the day or the morrow, the seasons that
>   laugh or that weep ;*
> *For these give joy and sadness ; but thou, Proserpina,
>   sleep.*

   Only two words have been changed, " seen " to " found,"
" sorrow " to " sadness ", yet the whole stanza seems
changed. Why ?

3. Suppose passage II went thus :

> *I have lived long enough, having seen*
> *One thing, that love hath an end ;*
> *Goddess and maiden and queen,*
> *Be near me now and befriend.*
> *Thou art more than the day or the morrow,*
> *The seasons that laugh or that weep ;*
> *For these give joy and sorrow ;*
> *But thou, Proserpina, sleep.*

   No word has been changed, but the stanza has been printed
in 8 lines (each of 3 feet) as suggested in note 1. Why
is the effect of the stanza so different ?

Notes : page 212.

18

PRACTICE IN INTERPRETATION

Read the following extract aloud :

I

From the forests and highlands
   We come, we come ;
From the river-girt islands,
   Where loud waves are dumb
     Listening to my sweet pipings.   5
The wind in the reeds, and the rushes,
   The bees on the bells of thyme,
The birds on the myrtle bushes,
   The cicale above in the lime,
And the lizards below in the grass,   10
Were as silent as ever old Tmolus was,
     Listening to my sweet pipings.

SHELLEY
(*Hymn of Pan*)

cicale : *chirping insects*
Tmolus : *mountain of Lydia*

I

1. Mr. de la Mare has said that the meaning of a poem or a line of poetry is the *whole* effect it has on us. Rhythm and rhyme, then, are part of the meaning. Why have they been treated separately ?

2. This poem is supposed to be sung by Pan, the God of " forests and highlands ", and " we " in the poem are Pan and the fauns and satyrs, his followers.
Line 2 : How do we come ? Are we walking or running, or dancing ?

3. In lines 1-4 there are two strong beats in each line.
In lines 6-10 there are three strong beats in each line.
In line 11 there are four strong beats.
How many beats are there in lines 5 and 12 ?

4. When you read this poem aloud what things especially help to make up the music of sound in it ?

Notes : page 213.

19

Read the following extracts aloud:

II

O bold majestic downs, smooth, fair and lonely;
O still solitude, only matched in the skies;
  Perilous in steep places,
  Soft in the level races,
Where sweeping in phantom silence the cloudland   5
    flies;
With lovely undulation of fall and rise;
  Entrenched with thickets thorned,
By delicate miniature dainty flowers adorned!

BRIDGES
(*The Downs*)

III

          A swan was there,
Beside a sluggish stream among the reeds.
It rose as he approached, and with strong wings
Scaling the upward sky, bent its bright course
High over the immeasurable main.

SHELLEY
(*Alastor*)

II

1. This is a most interesting stanza from the point of view of
   both rhythm and sound.
   How many strong accents are there in each line?
2. What accents do you give to " O " in line 1 and " O " in
   line 2?
3. What is the difference in rhythm between lines 3 and 4?
4. Draw up the rhyme scheme.
5. Lines 1-4. Point out any other sound effects in these
   lines.
6. Lines 5-8. Show that in each of these four lines the very
   sound of the words not only suits, but suggests the
   meaning of the line.

III

1. If you wish to see how much a poet can put into five lines,
   imagine that you are " he " in line 3, and describe all
   that you see and hear.
   Notes: page 214.

20

Read the following extract aloud:

IV

We are the music-makers,
  And we are the dreamers of dreams,
Wandering by lone sea-breakers,
  And sitting by desolate streams ;
World-losers and world-forsakers,   5
  On whom the pale moon gleams :
Yet we are the movers and shakers
  Of the world for ever, it seems.

O'SHAUGHNESSY
(*The Music-Makers*)

IV

1. What would be the effect of dropping " the " out of lines
   1 and 2 ?

2. If you have answered question 1, you should know who
   " we " are in lines 1 and 2, and what is meant by
   " makers " in line 1.

3. Do you believe the statement made in lines 7 and 8 ?

4. If they are the movers and shakers of the world, how can
   they be " world-losers and world-forsakers " ?

5. Lines 3-4. Is this just added for effect or is it a statement
   of fact ?

6. Note the stanza is one sentence. In what way is the effect
   of the stanza heightened
     (*a*) by the construction,
     (*b*) by the rhyme-scheme ?

Notes : page 215.

Read the following extract aloud:

V

I remember I once saw at sunset on a flat sandy shore, when the tide was low and the sea's roar came weighty and menacing from the distance, a great white sea-gull; it sat motionless, its silky bosom facing the crimson glow of the setting sun, and only now and then opening wide its great wings to greet the well-known sea, to greet the sinking lurid sun: I recalled it, as I heard Yakov.

TURGENEV
(*A Sportsman's Sketches*)

V

Turgenev, the great Russian writer, describing how the singing of Yakov affected him, wrote this passage.

1. Lines 1-7. In what way does this picture suggest the effect of music or poetry on us?

2. Does the sea-gull represent Yakov the singer, or Turgenev the listener?

3. Is there anything in this passage that recalls the poem " We are the music-makers "?

Notes : page 216.

GLYCINE'S SONG

A sunny shaft did I behold,
   From sky to earth it slanted :
And poised therein a bird so bold—
   Sweet bird, thou wert enchanted !

He sank, he rose, he twinkled, he trolled   5
   Within that shaft of sunny mist ;
His eyes of fire, his beak of gold,
   All else of amethyst !

And thus he sang : " Adieu ! adieu !
Love's dreams prove seldom true.   10
The blossoms they make no delay :
The sparkling dew-drops will not stay.
     Sweet month of May,
       We must away ;
         Far, far away !
           To-day ! to-day !

COLERIDGE
(1772-1834)

Swinburne says, "The song of Glycine flashes out like a visible sunbeam, it is one of the brightest bits of music ever done into words."

1. One of the chief faults in reading poetry is to read " with a slack imagination ". For instance, do you see clearly the picture with all its colour in stanza 2 ?

2. Which do you consider the most beautiful descriptive phrase in that stanza ?

3. The last four lines of stanza 3 are sometimes printed thus :

    Sweet month of May, we must away ;
    Far, far away ! to-day ! to-day !

Does this make any difference ?

Notes : page 216.

From THE SECOND BOOK OF KINGS
Chapter 19

Sennacherib, king of Assyria, sent the following message to Hezekiah, king of Judah :

10 Thus shall ye speak to Hezekiah king of Judah, saying, Let not thy God in whom thou trustest deceive thee, saying, Jerusalem shall not be delivered into the hand of the king of Assyria.
11 Behold, thou hast heard what the kings of Assyria have done to all lands, by destroying them utterly : and shalt thou be delivered ?
12 Have the gods of the nations delivered them which my fathers have destroyed ; as Gozan, and Haran, and Rezeph, and the children of Eden which were in Thelasar ?
13 Where is the king of Hamath, and the king of Arpad, and the king of the city of Sepharvaim, of Hena, and Ivah ?

But in reply, Isaiah the Prophet sent word to Hezekiah :

32 Therefore thus saith the Lord concerning the king of Assyria, He shall not come into this city, nor shoot an arrow there, nor come before it with shield, nor cast a bank against it.
33 By the way that he came, by the same shall he return, and shall not come into this city, saith the Lord.

And now the event :

35 And it came to pass that night, that the angel of the Lord went out, and smote in the camp of the Assyrians an hundred fourscore and five thousand : and when they arose early in the morning, behold, they were all dead corpses.

On this material the poet's " shaping spirit of imagination " works, and gives us the following poem :

THE DESTRUCTION OF SENNACHERIB

The Assyrian came down like the wolf on the fold,
And his cohorts were gleaming in purple and gold ;
And the sheen of their spears was like stars on the sea,
When the blue wave rolls nightly on deep Galilee.

Like the leaves of the forest when Summer is green,   5
That host with their banners at sunset were seen :
Like the leaves of the forest when Autumn hath blown,
That host on the morrow lay withered and strown.

For the Angel of Death spread his wings on the blast,
And breathed in the face of the foe as he passed ;   10
And the eyes of the sleepers waxed deadly and chill,
And their hearts but once heaved, and for ever grew
    still !

And there lay the steed with his nostril all wide,
But through it there rolled not the breath of his pride ;
And the foam of his gasping lay white on the turf,   15
And cold as the spray of the rock-beating surf.

And there lay the rider distorted and pale,
With the dew on his brow, and the rust on his mail ;
And the tents were all silent, the banners alone,
The lances unlifted, the trumpet unblown.   20

And the widows of Ashur are loud in their wail,
And the idols are broke in the temple of Baal ;
And the might of the Gentile, unsmote by the sword,
Hath melted like snow in the glance of the Lord !

   Ashur: *The Assyrians were said to be*   Byron
descended from Ashur, son of Shem.   (1788-1824)

1. What did Byron owe to the prose ? See " The Vision
   of Belshazzar ", Book III, page 130.
2. The poem is a series of great pictures. Use your imagination
   on them. Which of them are you most likely to remember ?
3. Did Sennacherib die ? Can you tell from the poem or the
   prose ?

Notes : page 217.

LOCK THE DOOR, LARISTON

" Lock the door, Lariston, lion of Liddesdale ;
Lock the door, Lariston, Lowther comes on ;
      The Armstrongs are flying,
      The widows are crying,
The Castletown's burning, and Oliver's gone !   5

" Lock the door, Lariston—high on the weather-gleam
See how the Saxon plumes bob on the sky—
      Yeoman and carbineer,
      Billman and halberdier,
Fierce is the foray, and far is the cry !   10

" Bewcastle brandishes high his broad scimitar ;
Ridley is riding his fleet-footed gray ;
      Hidley and Howard there,
      Wandale and Windermere ;
Lock the door, Lariston, hold them at bay.   15

" Why dost thou smile, noble Elliot of Lariston ?
Why does the joy-candle gleam in thine eye ?
      Thou bold Border ranger
      Beware of thy danger ;
Thy foes are relentless, determined, and nigh."   20

Jock Elliot raised up his steel bonnet and lookit,
His hand grasped the sword with a nervous embrace :
      " Ah, welcome, brave foemen,
      On earth there are no men
More gallant to meet in the foray or chase !   25

" Little know you of the hearts I have hidden here ;
Little know you of our moss-troopers' might—
      Linhope and Sorbie true,
      Sundhope and Milburn too,
Gentle in manner, but lions in fight !   30

" I have Mangerton, Ogilvie, Raeburn, and Netherbie.
Old Sim of Whitram, and all his array ;
      Come all Northumberland,
      Teesdale and Cumberland,
Here at the Breaken tower end shall the fray ! "   35

Scowled the broad sun o'er the links of green
      Liddesdale,
Red as the beacon-light tipped he the wold ;
      Many a bold martial eye
      Mirror'd that morning sky,
Never more oped on his orbit of gold.   40

Shrill was the bugle's note, dreadful the warrior's
      shout,
Lances and halberds in splinters were borne ;
      Helmet and hauberk then,
      Braved the claymore in vain,
Buckler and armlet in shivers were shorn.   45

See how they wane—the proud files of the Winder-
    mere !
Howard ! ah, woe to thy hopes of the day !
    Hear the wide welkin rend,
    While the Scots' shouts ascend—
" Elliot of Lariston, Elliot for aye ! "   50

HOGG
(1770-1835)

nervous : *sinewy, vigorous*

1. This poem divides naturally into **three** parts and each has
   its own atmosphere.

2. Contrast the rhythm of the long lines in this poem with
   those of stanzas I, II, III, in Practice in Rhythm, pages
   13-14.   In what way is the rhythm of this poem especially
   appropriate to the subject ?

3. The poem is full of sound as you would expect.   Why ?
   Contrast with the next poem.

4. What should be noted about the rhyme ?

5. (*a*) Which stanzas have no alliteration ?

   (*b*) Give two or three of the most effective uses of
   alliteration in the poem.

6. Give two or three of the words whose sound most strongly
   suggests the sense and so enforces the meaning.

7. Compare the first line with the last line.

8. The poem begins, " Lock the door, Lariston ".   Did he
   lock the door ?

Notes : page 218.

THE PATRIOT

It was roses, roses, all the way,
  With myrtle mixed in my path like mad :
The house-roofs seemed to heave and sway,
  The church-spires flamed, such flags they had,
A year ago on this very day.   5

The air broke into a mist with bells,
  The old walls rocked with the crowd and cries.
Had I said, " Good folks, mere noise repels—
  But give me your sun from yonder skies ! "
They had answered, " And afterward, what else ? " 10

Alack, it was I who leaped at the sun,
  To give it my loving friends to keep !
Nought man could do, have I left undone ɪ
  And you see my harvest, what I reap
This very day, now a year is run.   15

There's nobody on the house-tops now—
  Just a palsied few at the windows set—
For the best of the sight is, all allow,
  At the Shambles' Gate—or, better yet,
By the very scaffold's foot, I trow.   20

I go in the rain, and, more than needs,
  A rope cuts both my wrists behind ;
And I think, by the feel, my forehead bleeds,
  For they fling, whoever has a mind,
Stones at me for my year's misdeeds.   25

Thus I entered, and thus I go !
  In triumphs, people have dropped down dead.
" Paid by the world, what dost thou owe
  Me ? "—God might question ; now instead,
  'Tis God shall repay : I am safer so.   30

BROWNING
(1812-1889)

1. Read stanzas 1 and 2, then 4 and 5. If these formed the whole poem, which word in stanza 5 would you probably misinterpret ?

2. Stanza 6 gives the key to the poem. " Thus I entered (*i.e.* stanzas 1 and 2) and thus I go ! " " In triumphs, people have dropped down dead." Would it have been better for him if he had dropped down dead in his triumph " a year ago on this very day " ?

3. Now you should be ready to tackle the only stanza in the poem which troubles some people, stanza 3. In this stanza what is the " sun " (line 1) and who are " my loving friends " (line 2) ?

4. Why was he being put to death ?

5. (*a*) Why did the people hate him so ?

   (*b*) In which line do you feel the hatred most ?

6. We attend less to the sound of this poem than we did to that of " Lock the Door, Lariston ". Why ?

Notes : page 219.

TO THE MUSES

Whether on Ida's shady brow
  Or in the chambers of the East,
The chambers of the Sun, that now
  From ancient melody have ceased;

Whether in heaven ye wander fair,   5
  Or the green corners of the earth,
Or the blue regions of the air
  Where the melodious winds have birth;

Whether on crystal rocks ye rove,
  Beneath the bosom of the sea,   10
Wandering in many a coral grove;
  Fair Nine, forsaking Poetry;

How have you left the ancient love
  That bards of old enjoy'd in you!
The languid strings do scarcely move,   15
  The sound is forced, the notes are few.

BLAKE
(1757-1827)

1. In which lines do you find the main statement in this poem?

2. If you try to build up the main thought of this poem into one prose sentence, avoiding all repetition, and, to save space, summing up all the " whether " clauses into the one word " wheresoever ", how much do you draw from each stanza?

3. In this poem of four stanzas practically all the main thought is in the fourth. How does this affect our enjoyment of the other three?

4. Have you learned anything from answering questions 1, 2, and 3?

5. Blake's style is famous for its simplicity and sweetness. In which stanza of this poem are simplicity and sweetness most clearly felt?

6. This poem was written about 1790. Does this help us to understand it?

Notes : page 220.

31

From THE LOTOS-EATERS

There is sweet music here that softer falls
Than petals from blown roses on the grass,
Or night-dews on still waters between walls
Of shadowy granite, in a gleaming pass ;
Music that gentlier on the spirit lies,   5
Than tir'd eyelids upon tir'd eyes ;
Music that brings sweet sleep down from the
  blissful skies.
Here are cool mosses deep,
And thro' the moss the ivies creep,
And in the stream the long-leaved flowers weep, 10
And from the craggy ledge the poppy hangs in
  sleep.

TENNYSON
(1809-1892)

1. Lines 8-11 have already been fully treated in " Practice
 in Rhyme " (pages 17 and 211)

2. Lines 1-7 form one sentence, and the principal clause is
 in the first line. Is this a badly constructed sentence ?
 See notes 3 and 4 to the last poem (page 220).

3. Which are the most frequently quoted lines in this stanza ?

4. This poem should be compared with the passages on Music
 in Book III (pages 67-74).

Notes : page 221.

THE DOWNS

O bold majestic downs, smooth, fair and lonely;
O still solitude, only matched in the skies;
   Perilous in steep places,
   Soft in the level races,
Where sweeping in phantom silence the cloudland
    flies;   5
With lovely undulation of fall and rise;
   Entrenched with thickets thorned,
By delicate miniature dainty flowers adorned!

I climb your crown, and lo! a sight surprising
Of sea in front uprising, steep and wide: 10
   And scattered ships ascending
   To heaven, lost in the blending
Of distant blues, where water and sky divide,
Urging their engines against wind and tide,
   And all so small and slow   15
They seem to be wearily pointing the way they would go.

The accumulated murmur of soft plashing,
Of waves on rocks dashing and searching the sands,
   Takes my ear, in the veering
   Baffled wind, as rearing   20
Upright at the cliff, to the gullies and rifts he stands;
And his conquering surges scour out over the lands;
   While again at the foot of the downs
He masses his strength to recover the topmost crowns.

ROBERT BRIDGES
(*20th Century*)

1. The first stanza of this poem has already been treated in
   " Practice in Interpretation " (pages 20 and 214). It
   would be well to re-read these questions and notes
   before answering the following.

2. The rhyme scheme of stanza 1 is given on page 214, note 4.
   Are the rhyme schemes of stanzas 2 and 3 exactly the
   same?

3. Does the fact that lines 3 and 4 are short have any effect
   upon line 5?   Apply this also to lines 11, 12, and 13,
   and to lines 19, 20, and 21.

4. Can you see the " sight surprising " referred to in line 9?
   What is surprising about it?

5. Apply what was said regarding lines 5-8 on page 20 to
   lines 16 and 17.

6. Have you learned anything about Bridges' method of
   writing from your study of this poem?   Compare the
   style with that of the next poem.

   Notes : page 222

TO VIOLETS

Welcome, maids of honour !
   You do bring
   In the spring,
And wait upon her.

She has virgins many,   5
   Fresh and fair ;
   Yet you are
More sweet than any.

You're the maiden posies,
   And so graced   10
   To be placed
'Fore damask roses.

Yet, though thus respected,
   By and by
   Ye do lie,   15
Poor girls, neglected.

HERRICK
(1591-1674)

1. From the appearance of the above poem, one would say that each stanza consisted of two short lines, lines 2 and 3, and two longer lines, lines 1 and 4. How many beats are there in each line of stanza 1 ?

2. How many words in each stanza have more than one syllable ?
What do you learn from answering this question ?

3. Does the style suit the subject of this poem ?

4. In what way does the last line take us back to the first ?

5. Compare this poem with the last. Which would be the easier to write ?

Notes : page 223.

BESSIE BELL AND MARY GRAY

O Bessie Bell and Mary Gray,
   They were twa bonnie lasses ;
They biggit a bower on yon burn-brae,
   And theekit it owre wi' rashes.

They theekit it owre wi' rashes green,   5
   They theekit it owre wi' heather ;
But the pest cam frae the burrows-town
   And slew them baith thegither.

They thought to lie in Methven kirk-yard,
   Amang their noble kin ;   10
But they maun lie in Stronach Haugh,
   To beik fornent the sin.

And Bessie Bell and Mary Gray,
   They were twa bonnie lasses ;
They biggit a bower on yon burn-brae,   15
   And theekit it owre wi' rashes.

ANONYMOUS

biggit : *built*   theekit : *thatched*
burn-brae : *bank of a stream*   rashes : *rushes*
burrows-town : *town*   pest : *plague*
Haugh : *low ground beside a stream*
beik fornent the sin : *bask before the sun (lie unburied)*

1. If you have read Books II and III of this series, you already know something about the ballads. What qualities of the old ballads do you find in this poem ?

2. Why does the poet not make more of the story ?

3. The fourth stanza is an exact repetition of the first, yet the effect of the stanza and the manner in which we read it are different. Why ?

Notes : page 224.

BONNIE GEORGE CAMPBELL

Hie upon Hielands,
   And laigh upon Tay,
Bonnie George Campbell
   Rade out on a day.

Saddled and bridled   5
   And booted rade he;
Hame cam his guid horse,
   But never cam he.

Down cam his mother dear,
   Greetin' fu' sair,   10
And down cam his bonnie bride,
   Rivin' her hair:

" The meadow lies green,
   And the corn is unshorn,
The barn is to build   15
   And my babe is unborn."

Saddled and bridled
   And booted rade he;
A plume in his helmet,
   A sword at his knee.   20

Toom cam his saddle
   All bloody to see:
Oh, hame cam his guid horse
   But never cam he.

Anonymous

laigh: *low*   greetin': *weeping*
rivin': *tearing*   toom: *empty*

1. In what ways does this resemble the previous poem?
2. Compare the rhythm of this poem with that of the preceding one.
3. Who speaks in stanza 4?

   Notes: page 225.

THE LAMENT OF THE BORDER WIDOW

My love he built me a bonnie bower,
And clad it a' wi' lilye flour ;
A brawer bower ye ne'er did see,
Than my true love he built for me.

There came a man, by middle day,   5
He spied his sport, and went away ;
And brought the King that very night,
Who brake my bower, and slew my knight.

He slew my knight, to me sae dear ;
He slew my knight, and poined his gear ;   10
My servants all for life did flee,
And left me in extremitie.

I sewed his sheet, making my mane ;
I watched the corpse, myself alane ;
I watched his body, night and day ;   15
No living creature came that way.

I took his body on my back,
And whiles I gaed, and whiles I sat ;
I digged a grave, and laid him in,
And happed him with the sod sae green.   20

But think na ye my heart was sair,
When I laid the moul' on his yellow hair ;
O think na ye my heart was wae,
When I turn'd about, away to gae ?

Nae living man I'll love again,
Since that my lovely knight is slain;
Wi' ae lock of his yellow hair
I'll chain my heart for evermair.

25

ANONYMOUS

poined : *seized*   moul' : *earth*

1. What is the full significance of line 12 ?

2. Stanza 5. This stanza is almost stark in its simplicity. It reads like a list of facts. What is it that gives it such wonderful pathos ?

3. In all she had to do : (*a*) What do you think hurt her most ? (*b*) When did she feel her loneliness most ?

4. (*a*) If the story were not so sad, we should not know the real greatness of her character.

   (*b*) If she were not a woman of so great a character, the story would not be so sad.

   Are these two statements true ?

5. Is this a sad poem ?

   Notes : page 225.

HELEN OF KIRKCONNEL

I wish I were where Helen lies!
Night and day on me she cries;
Oh that I were where Helen lies,
   On fair Kirkconnel lea!

Curst be the heart that thought the thought,   5
And curst the hand that fired the shot,
When in my arms burd Helen dropt,
   And died to succour me!

Oh think na ye my heart was sair,
When my Love dropp'd and spak nae mair!   10
There did she swoon wi' meikle care,
   On fair Kirkconnel lea.

As I went down the water-side,
None but my foe to be my guide,
None but my foe to be my guide,   15
   On fair Kirkconnel lea;

I lighted down my sword to draw,
I hackéd him in pieces sma,
I hackéd him in pieces sma,
   For her sake that died for me.   20

Oh Helen fair, beyond compare!
I'll mak a garland o' thy hair,
Shall bind my heart for evermair
   Until the day I die!

Oh that I were where Helen lies!   25
Night and day on me she cries;
Out of my bed she bids me rise,
   Says, " Haste, and come to me!"

Oh Helen fair! Oh Helen chaste!
If I were with thee, I'd be blest,
Where thou lies low and tak's thy rest,   30
  On fair Kirkconnel lea.

I wish my grave were growing green,
A winding-sheet drawn owre my een,
And I in Helen's arms lying,
  On fair Kirkconnel lea.   35

I wish I were where Helen lies!
Night and day on me she cries;
And I am weary of the skies,
  For her sake that died for me.   40

ANONYMOUS

burd : *a lady*

1. Note the effect of the repetition and variations in stanzas
   1, 7 and 10.

2. If you wish to understand the wonderful effects a poet
   can produce by merely repeating a line, read the following
   and compare carefully with stanzas 4 and 5 :

   > *As I went down the water-side,*
   > *None but my foe to be my guide,*
   >   *On fair Kirkconnel lea ;*
   >
   > *I lighted down my sword to draw,*
   > *I hackéd him in pieces sma'*
   >   *For her sake that died for me.*

3. The whole story is told in stanzas 1-5. What would be
   the effect of omitting stanzas 6-10 ?

4. Show how this poem resembles and differs from " The
   Lament of the Border Widow ".

5. Is this a sad poem ?

Notes : page 226.

EDWARD, EDWARD

" Why does your brand sae drap wi' bluid,
        Edward, Edward ;
Why does your brand sae drap wi' bluid,
  And why sae sad gang ye, O ? "
" O I hae kill'd my hawk sae guid,   5
        Mither, mither ;
O I hae kill'd my hawk sae guid,
  And I had nae mair but he, O."

" Your hawk's bluid was never sae red,
        Edward, Edward ;   10
Your hawk's bluid was never sae red,
  My dear son, I tell thee, O."
" O I hae kill'd my red-roan steed,
        Mither, mither ;
O I hae kill'd my red-roan steed,   15
  That erst was sae fair and free, O."

" Your steed was auld, and ye hae got mair,
        Edward, Edward ;
Your steed was auld, and ye hae got mair ;
  Some other dule ye dree, O."   20
" O I hae kill'd my father dear,
        Mither, mither ;
O I hae kill'd my father dear,
  Alas, and wae is me, O ! "

"And whatten penance will ye dree for that,   25
        Edward, Edward ;
And whatten penance will ye dree for that,
    My dear son, now tell me, O ? "
" I'll set my feet in yonder boat,
        Mither, mither ;   30
I'll set my feet in yonder boat,
    And I'll fare over the sea, O."

" And what will ye do wi' your towers and your ha',
        Edward, Edward ;
And what will ye do wi' your towers and your ha',   35
    That were sae fair to see, O ? "
" I'll let them stand till they down fa',
        Mither, mither ;
I'll let them stand till they down fa',
    For here never mair maun I be, O."   40

" And what will ye leave to your bairns and your wife,
        Edward, Edward ;
And what will ye leave to your bairns and your wife,
    When ye gang over the sea, O ? "
" The warld's room : let them beg through life ;   45
        Mither, mither ;
The warld's room : let them beg through life ;
    For hame never mair will I see, O."

" And what will ye leave to your ain mither dear,
      Edward, Edward ;   50
And what will ye leave to your ain mither dear,
  My dear son, now tell me, O ? "
" The curse of hell frae me shall ye bear,
      Mither, mither ;
The curse of hell frae me shall ye bear :   55
  Sic counsels ye gave to me, O ! "

ANONYMOUS

brand : *sword*   dule : *grief*   dree : *suffer*

This poem reads like a short scene from a great tragic drama. What went before the scene, what was to follow, we can only surmise. There may therefore be differences of opinion regarding the characters of Edward and his mother. If after reading my views you decide I am wrong, hold to your own opinion. Your disagreement with me may help to confirm and clarify your own view of the poem. See page 12.

1. The mother must have known what had happened whenever Edward entered with his dripping brand, and looking " sae sad ".
Why, then, did she ask the first question ?

2. What things in the poem help us to form an idea of the character of the mother ?

3. Lines 5-8 and 13-16. Why does Edward not tell the truth at once ?

4. Lines 45-8. Has Edward no love for his wife and children ?

5. Which lines in this poem would be the most difficult to read ?

6. How is it that we can enjoy reading a poem like this ?

   Notes : page 227.

44

THE OLD CLOAK

This winter's weather it waxeth cold,
And frost it freezeth on every hill,
And Boreas blows his blast so bold
That all our cattle are like to spill.
Bell, my wife, she loves not strife;
She said unto me quietlye,
" Rise up, and save cow Crumbock's life.
Man, put thine old cloak about thee ! "

He :   O Bell, my wife, why dost thou flyte?
Thou kens my cloak is very thin :   10
It is so bare and overworn,
A crické thereon cannot renn.
Then I'll no longer borrow nor lend;
For once I'll new apparell'd be;
To-morrow I'll to town and spend;   15
For I'll have a new cloak about me.

She :   Cow Crumbock is a very good cow;
She has been always true to the pail;
She has helped us to butter and cheese, I trow,
And other things she will not fail.   20
I would be loth to see her pine,
Good husband, counsel take of me :
It is not for us to go so fine—
Man, take thine old cloak about thee !

He :　My cloak it was a very good cloak,　　　25
　　　　It hath been always true to the wear ;
　　　　But now it is not worth a groat :
　　　　I have had it four and forty year.
　　　　Sometime it was of cloth in grain :
　　　　'Tis now but a sigh clout, as you may see :　　30
　　　　It will neither hold out wind nor rain ;
　　　　And I'll have a new cloak about me.

She :　It is four and forty years ago
　　　　Since the one of us the other did ken ;
　　　　And we have had, betwixt us two,　　　35
　　　　Of lads and bonnie lassies ten :
　　　　We have brought them up to women and men :
　　　　In the fear of God I trow they be :
　　　　And why wilt thou thyself misken ?
　　　　Man, take thine old cloak about thee !　　　40

He :　O Bell, my wife, why dost thou flyte ?
　　　　Now is now, and then was then :
　　　　Seek now all the world throughout,
　　　　Thou kens not clowns from gentlemen :
　　　　They are clad in black, green, yellow, and blue,　45
　　　　So far above their own degree.
　　　　Once in my life I'll take the view ;
　　　　For I'll have a new cloak about me.

She : King Stephen was a worthy peer ;
His breeches cost him but a crown ;   50
He held them sixpence all too dear,
And called the tailor thieving loon.
He was a king and wore a crown,
And thou'se but of a low degree ;
It's pride that puts this country down :   55
Man, take thine old cloak about thee !

He :   Bell, my wife, she loves not strife,
Yet she will lead me if she can ;
And to maintain an easy life
I oft must yield, though I'm good-man.   60
It's not for a man with a woman to threap
Unless he first give o'er the plea :
As we began, so will we keep,
And I'll take my old cloak about me.

ANONYMOUS

Boreas : *North Wind*   sigh clout : *rag for straining*
spill : *die*   *liquids*
flyte : *scold*   loon : *low fellow*
crické : *cricket*   threap : *argue*
cloth in grain : *scarlet cloth*

1. Coming to this poem after the last, we feel at once its
   homely, kindly, humorous atmosphere. The last was a
   tragedy ; this is a comedy, and the more carefully we
   examine it, the more delightful a comedy we find it
   Compare the construction of this poem with that of the
   last.

2. What exactly is the point at issue ?

   Notes : page 229

47

THERE WAS A KNICHT

There was a knicht riding **frae the** east,
    Jennifer gentle an' rosemaree.
Who had been wooing at monie a place,
    As the doo flies owre the mulberry tree.

He cam unto a widow's door,
And speird where her three dochters were.

" The auldest ane's to a washing gane,
The second's to a bleaching gane.

" The youngest ane's to a wedding gane,
And it will be nicht or they be hame."

He sat him doun upon a stane,
Till the three lasses cam tripping hame.

The auldest ane she let him in,
And barred the door wi' a siller pin.

The second ane she made his bed,
And laid saft pillows under his head.

The youngest ane was bauld and bricht,
And she tarried for words wi' this stranger knicht.

" Gin ye will answer me questions ten,
The morn ye sall be made my ain :

" O what is higher nor the tree ?
And what is deeper nor the sea ?

" Or what is heavier nor the lead ?
And what is better nor the bread ?

" Or what is whiter nor the milk ?
Or what is safter nor the silk ?

" Or what is sharper nor a thorn?
Or what is louder nor a horn?

" Or what is greener nor the grass?
Or what is waur nor a woman was?"   30

" O heaven is higher nor the tree,
And hell is deeper nor the sea.

" O sin is heavier nor the lead,
The blessing's better nor the bread.

" The snaw is whiter nor the milk,   35
And the down is safter nor the silk.

" Hunger is sharper nor a thorn,
And shame is louder nor a horn.

" The pies are greener nor the grass,
And Clootie's waur nor a woman was."   40

As sune as she the fiend did name,
     Jennifer gentle an' rosemaree,
He flew awa' in a blazing flame,
     As the doo flies owre the mulberry tree.

ANONYMOUS

doo : *dove*	or : *before*	waur : *worse*
speird : *asked*	unco : *strange*	pies : *magpies*

It was an old belief that Satan went about not only like
a roaring lion, but in many other disguises, such as " the
demon lover " or " knicht " of the above poem, and the
" fause knicht " of the next. It was also held that you were
safe from him so long as you faced him, answered all his
questions, and, if possible, had the last word. It was fatal
to give way to him.

1. Is the lady afraid of the knight?

2. Which phrase gives you the tone or atmosphere of the
     poem?

3. Compare this poem with the one following.
     Notes : page 230.

49

THE FAUSE KNICHT UPON THE ROAD

"O where are ye gaun?"
  Quo' the fause knicht upon the road:
"I'm gaun to the schule,"
  Quo' the wee boy, and still he stood.

"What is that upon your back?"
  Quo' the fause knicht upon the road:
"Atweel it is my books,"
  Quo' the wee boy, and still he stood.

"What's that ye've got in your arm?"
  Quo' the fause knicht upon the road:
"Atweel it is my peat,"
  Quo' the wee boy, and still he stood.

"Wha's aucht the sheep?"
  Quo' the fause knicht upon the road:
"They're mine and my mither's,"
  Quo' the wee boy, and still he stood.

"How monie o' them are mine?"
  Quo' the fause knicht upon the road:
"A' they that hae blue tails,"
  Quo' the wee boy, and still he stood.

"I wish ye were on yon tree,"
  Quo' the fause knicht upon the road:
"And a good ladder under me,"
  Quo' the wee boy, and still he stood.

"And the ladder for to break,"
  Quo' the fause knicht upon the road:
"And you for to fa' down,"
  Quo' the wee boy, and still he stood.

"I wish ye were in yon sea,"
    Quo' the fause knicht upon the road :   30
"And a good bottom under me."
    Quo' the wee boy, and still he stood.

"And the bottom for to break,"
    Quo' the fause knicht upon the road :
"And you to be drowned,"   35
    Quo' the wee boy, and still he stood.

ANONYMOUS

atweel : *truly*   wha's aucht : *who owns*
peat : *for the school-room fire*   bottom : *ship*
See the note on page 49

1. Is the " wee boy " afraid of the " fause knicht " ?

2. There is a phrase which occurs in every stanza of the
   poem and which seems to give the tone or atmosphere
   of the whole. Can you find it ?

3. In the preceding poem, the knight's questions come one
   after another, lines 21-30, as did the lady's replies, lines
   31-40. In this poem we have question and answer
   alternately right through the poem. Which is the better
   method ?

4. If one of these two poems was written before the other,
   which seems to you the earlier ?

5. Which seems to you the more like truth ?

6. Which do you prefer ?

   Notes : page 230.

JENNY KISSED ME

Jenny kissed me when we met,
  Jumping from the chair she sat in ;
Time, you thief, who love to get
  Sweets into your list, put that in !
Say I'm weary, say I'm sad,   5
  Say that health and wealth have missed me,
Say I'm growing old, but add,
  Jenny kissed me.

HUNT
(1784-1859)

DON'T ASK FOR A KISS

Don't ask for a kiss ;
  She would have to refuse you.
Take my tip in this,
Don't ask for a kiss,
Just make sure you don't miss,   5
  And I'm sure she'll excuse you.
Don't ask for a kiss ;
  She would have to refuse you.

GEORGE A. C. MacKINLAY
(20th Century)

It will be of interest to state that Jenny was Jane Welsh Carlyle, the wife of the author of " Sartor Resartus ", and that the incident recorded occurred after hearing Leigh Hunt read his sonnet, " On a Lock of Milton's Hair ".

1. Wherein lies the charm of these two poems ?

2. Note the form of the second poem ; lines 1, 4, and 7 are the same, so are 2 and 8. Now suppose we try to write a triolet, as this poem is called. As we are not poets, we want all the help possible. We begin with a simple statement made by a sister to her brother, such as, " My ankle is sore, so I don't want to hurry ". Will you try to complete it ?

Notes : page 231.

WHY SO PALE AND WAN, FOND LOVER?

Why so pale and wan, fond lover?
  Prithee, why so pale?
Will, when looking well can't move her,
  Looking ill prevail?
  Prithee, why so pale?   5

Why so dull and mute, young sinner?
  Prithee, why so mute?
Will, when speaking well can't win her,
  Saying nothing do't?
  Prithee, why so mute?   10

Quit, quit for shame! This will not move;
  This cannot take her.
If of herself she will not love,
  Nothing can make her:
  The devil take her!   15

fond: *foolish*   SUCKLING
(1609-1642)

1. How would you read stanzas 1 and 2?

2. How would you read stanza 3?

3. In stanzas 1 and 2, line 5 is a repetition of line 2, which
is itself a repetition of part of the question in line 1, *e.g.*

Stanza 1, line 1. *Why so pale?*
           2. *Prithee, why so pale?*
           5. *Prithee, why so pale?*

Thus it seems we might omit lines 2 and 5. Here is
the stanza without them:

Why so pale and wan, fond lover?
Will, when looking well can't move her,
Looking ill prevail?

Now we have evidently lost the charming, yet quaint
rhythm and rhyme, and in this poem they are very
important. Have we lost anything else?

4. In stanza 3 there are certain changes in rhythm. What
effect have these on the tone and feeling of the
stanza?

Notes: page 232.

TO THE VIRGINS, TO MAKE MUCH OF TIME

Gather ye rosebuds while ye may,
  Old Time is still a-flying :
And this same flower that smiles to-day
  To-morrow will be dying.

The glorious lamp of heaven, the sun,   5
  The higher he's a-getting,
The sooner will his race be run,
  And nearer he's to setting.

That age is best which is the first,
  When youth and blood are warmer ;   10
But being spent, the worse, and worst
  Times still succeed the former.

Then be not coy, but use your time,
  And while ye may, go marry ;
For having lost but once your prime,   15
  You may for ever tarry.

HERRICK
(1591-1674)

1. This is, perhaps, the best known of Herrick's lyrics.
Certainly the first line is his best known line. The
theme is a favourite with him. Compare the following
lines from his " Corinna's going a-Maying " :

> *Come, let us go, while we are in our prime,*
> *And take the harmless folly of the time.*
>   *We shall grow old apace, and die*
>   *Before we know our liberty.*
>   *Our life is short, and our days run*
>   *As fast away as does the sun.* . . .
> *Then, while time serves, and we are but decaying,*
> *Come, my Corinna, come, let's go a-Maying.*

The same theme is treated in these lines from Spenser :

> *Gather therefore the Rose whilest yet is prime,*
> *For soone comes age that will her pride deflowre ;*
> *Gather the Rose of love whilest yet is time.*
>
> *" The Faerie Queene," Book II, 12 and 25*

and in the following stanza from Fitzgerald's " The Rubaiyat of Omar Khayyám " :

> *" Alas, that Spring should vanish with the Rose !*
> *That Youth's sweet-scented Manuscript should close !*
> *The Nightingale that in the Branches sang,*
> *Ah, whence, and whither flown again, who knows ! "*

2. One stanza of this poem you read differently from the other three. Which, and why ?

3. What is it that charms you so much in this lyric ?

4. What effect does the double rhyme of the second and fourth lines of each stanza have on the rhythm ?

Notes : page 233.

FOUR SONGS FROM SHAKESPEARE

SIGH NO MORE, LADIES

Sigh no more, ladies, sigh no more,
  Men were deceivers ever;
One foot in sea, and one on shore,
  To one thing constant never.
      Then sigh not so,   5
      But let them go,
  And be you blithe and bonny,
Converting all your sounds of woe
  Into Hey nonny, nonny.

Sing no more ditties, sing no mo   10
  Of dumps so dull and heavy;
The fraud of men was ever so,
  Since summer first was leavy.
      Then sigh not so,
      But let them go,   15
  And be you blithe and bonny,
Converting all your sounds of woe
  Into Hey nonny, nonny.

O MISTRESS MINE

O Mistress mine, where are you roaming?
O, stay and hear! your true love's coming,
  That can sing both high and low:
Trip no further, pretty sweeting;
Journeys end in lovers' meeting,   5
  Every wise man's son doth know.

What is love? 'tis not hereafter;
Present mirth hath present laughter;
  What's to come is still unsure:
In delay there lies no plenty;   10
Then come kiss me, sweet-and-twenty!
  Youth's a stuff will not endure.

It was a lover and his lass,
    With a hey, and a ho, and a hey nonino,
That o'er the green corn-field did pass,
    In the spring time, the only pretty ring time,
When birds do sing, hey ding a ding, ding;   5
Sweet lovers love the spring.

Between the acres of the rye,
    With a hey, and a ho, and a hey nonino,
These pretty country folks would lie,
    In the spring time, the only pretty ring time,   10
When birds do sing, hey ding a ding, ding;
Sweet lovers love the spring.

This carol they began that hour,
    With a hey, and a ho, and a hey nonino,
How that life was but a flower   15
    In the spring time, the only pretty ring time,
When birds do sing, hey ding a ding, ding;
Sweet lovers love the spring.

And, therefore, take the present time
    With a hey, and a ho, and a hey nonino,   20
For love is crownéd with the prime
    In the spring time, the only pretty ring time,
When birds do sing, hey ding a ding, ding;
Sweet lovers love the spring.

HARK! HARK! THE LARK

Hark! hark! the lark at heaven's gate sings,
  And Phoebus 'gins arise,
His steeds to water at those springs
  On chaliced flowers that lies;
And winking Mary-buds begin   5
  To ope their golden eyes;
With everything that pretty is,
  My lady sweet, arise!
     Arise, arise!

SHAKESPEARE
(1564-1616)

Shakespeare wrote these songs to be sung in his plays. He intended that we should hear them sung, not spoken. As we have them in this book, therefore, they are robbed of part of their charm. They are printed here, because the words have a wonderful charm in themselves, and, once you realise that, you will enjoy the songs all the more when you hear them sung.

I. *Sigh no more, Ladies.*

1. Lines 2 and 7. Which of these lines gives you the atmosphere of the song?

2. Lines 5 and 6. These two lines are often printed as one, thus:

> *Then sigh not so, but let them go.*

Which form do you prefer?

II. *O Mistress Mine.*

3. Which two lines give best the atmosphere of the song?

4. In what way does the atmosphere of II differ from I?

III. *It was a Lover and his Lass.*

5. In stanzas 2, 3 and 4, lines 1 and 3 are new, while lines
   2, 4, 5 and 6 are repeated from the first stanza.   Here
   are the eight lines without the repetition.

> *It was a lover and his lass,*
> *That o'er the green corn-field did pass.*
> *Between the acres of the rye,*
> *These pretty country folks would lie.*
> *This carol they began that hour,*
> *How that life was but a flower.*
> *And, therefore, take the present time,*
> *For love is crownéd with the prime.*

What is the effect of leaving out the repetitions?

IV. *Hark! Hark! the Lark.*

6. Line 1.   Compare with this line, the following lines from
   one of Shakespeare's sonnets :

> *Yet in these thoughts myself almost despising,*
> *Haply I think on thee—and then my state,*
> *Like to the lark at break of day arising*
> *From sullen earth, sings hymns at heaven's gate.*

7. Lines 2-4.   What do these lines mean?

8. Lines 4-7 are sometimes printed thus :

> *And winking Mary-buds begin to ope their golden eyes ;*
> *With everything that pretty is, my lady sweet, arise.*

Which form do you prefer?

9 Why do you think these four songs are grouped together?
   Do you approve of the order in which they are given?

Notes : page 234.

THE SOLITARY REAPER

Behold her, single in the field,
Yon solitary Highland Lass!
Reaping and singing by herself;
Stop here, or gently pass!
Alone she cuts and binds the grain,   5
And sings a melancholy strain;
O listen! for the Vale profound
Is overflowing with the sound.

No Nightingale did ever chaunt
More welcome notes to weary bands   10
Of travellers in some shady haunt,
Among Arabian sands:
A voice so thrilling ne'er was heard
In spring-time from the Cuckoo-bird,
Breaking the silence of the seas   15
Among the farthest Hebrides.

Will no one tell me what she sings?—
Perhaps the plaintive numbers flow
For old, unhappy, far-off things,
And battles long ago: 20
Or is it some more humble lay,
Familiar matter of to-day?
Some natural sorrow, loss, or pain.
That has been, and may be again?

Whate'er the theme, the Maiden sang   25
As if her song could have no ending;
I saw her singing at her work,
And o'er the sickle bending;—
I listened, motionless and still;
And, as I mounted up the hill,   30
The music in my heart I bore,
Long after it was heard no more.

WORDSWORTH
(1770-1850)

1. You will notice that stanzas 1 and 4 would make a complete
   little poem without the other two; in fact, they join
   up so well when printed one after another, that, had
   you not read the whole poem, you could not have told
   anything had been omitted. In stanza 2 Wordsworth
   tells us how much the song appeals to him, and in
   stanza 3 he tries to suggest what the girl may be singing
   about. Excluding these two stanzas, how often does
   he tell us that the girl is alone, that she is reaping and
   that she is singing?

2. What do we know about the girl herself, the scene, the
   story?

3. What part of the picture do stanzas 1 and 4 form?

4. What made the song so welcome and thrilling to Words-
   worth?

5. In this poem there are two couplets that everyone wishes
   to remember. One I have given in note 4. Can you
   find the other?

   Notes: page 235

THE QUEEN OF LOCHLIN

Aillte (pronounce Isle-shū) one of the handsomest of
Fingal's young warriors, hurt that his chief had apparently
slighted him, fled to the court of the King of Lochlin
(Norway) and took service with him. But here love smote the
Queen and Aillte, and together they escaped **and sought**
the protection of Fingal.

The Queen of Lochlin of the brown shields
Deep love gave, that all endureth,
To Aillte, young, of the keen edg'd blades,
And secretly with him fled she.

The King of Lochlin his hardy hosts   5
In this hour of need gather'd,
And with them came the mighty stalwarts
Of nine kings from the northern shores.

There were that wounded fell or died on the field of
    battle,
But never one was home returning of all the mighty
    Lochlin men.   10

OSSIAN

1. This reminds us of the story of Helen of Troy with a
   different ending. Do you sympathise only with the
   lovers here ?

2. " Love, Strife, Death, and that which is beyond Death.
   These are, it would seem, definitely the four themes
   about which our earliest bards sang."

PROFESSOR GILBERT MURRAY.

On the next page you will find a prose translation of a
passage from the Anglo-Saxon poem, " Beowulf",
telling of the burial of Scyld.

Note : page 236.

From BEOWULF

Scyld, the poet tells us, arrived as a little boy, alone and destitute, on the shores of the Danes ; he became their king, a great and glorious chief, beloved by his loyal people ; he conquered many tribes beyond the sea ; he was blessed with a son ; and when at the fated hour he had passed away, he was sent out into the sea with all the pomp of military splendour.

KLAEBER

Then, at the fated hour, Scyld, full of exploits, departed to go into the keeping of the Lord. Then did they, his dear comrades, bear him out to the shore of the sea, as he himself had besought them, whilst he, Protector of the Scyldings, loved lord of the land, long ruled by his word.

There at the haven stood the ring-prowed vessel, the prince's ship, glittering with ice, ready for the outward-bound. They laid then the beloved chieftain, the bestower of rings, on the bosom of the ship, the glorious hero by the mast. There were brought many treasures, ornaments from far-off lands. Never have I known a ship more fairly fitted out with war weapons and battle trappings, swords and coats of mail. Upon his breast lay many treasures which were to travel far with him into the possession of the flood. Certainly they furnished him with no less of gifts, of tribal-treasures, than did those who sent him forth in the beginning, while he was still a child, alone over the waves. Moreover they set besides a golden banner high above his head, and let the flood bear him away, gave him to the deep. Sad was their soul, sorrowful their spirit. No man can tell for certain, no chief of council nor hero under heaven, who received that burden.

" Beowulf ", *Lines* 26-52

Will no one tell me what she sings ?—
Perhaps the plaintive numbers flow
For old, unhappy, far-off things,
And battles long ago.

63

THE COUNTRY OF THE CAMISARDS

We travelled in the print of olden wars,
    Yet all the land was green,
    And love we found, and peace,
    Where fire and war had been.

They pass and smile, the children of the sword—   5
    No more the sword they wield ;
    And O, how deep the corn
    Along the battlefield !

R. L. STEVENSON
(1850-1894)

Camisards : *Protestants of the Cevennes*

OLD BATTLE-FIELD

Old battle-field, fresh with spring flowers again—
    All that is left of the dream
    Of twice ten thousand warriors slain.

Old Japanese Poem

THE FIELD OF WATERLOO

Stop ! for thy tread is on an Empire's dust !
An earthquake's spoil is sepulchred below !
Is the spot mark'd with no colossal bust ?
Nor column trophied for triumphal show ?
None ; but the moral's truth tells simpler so.   5
As the ground was before, thus let it be ;
How that red rain hath made the harvest grow !
And is this all the world has gain'd by thee,
Thou first and last of fields ! king-making Victory !

"Childe Harold's Pilgrimage", *Canto III, Stanza XVII.*

BYRON
(1788-1824)

Contrast the spirit of these three poems.

    Notes : page 236.

A SONG OF SOLDIERS

As I sat musing by the frozen dyke,
There was one man marching with a bright steel
    pike,
Marching in the dayshine like a ghost came he,
And behind me was the moaning and the murmur of
    the sea.

As I sat musing, 'twas not one but ten—   5
Rank on rank of ghostly soldiers marching o'er the
    fen,
Marching in the misty air they showed in dreams to
    me,
And behind me was the shouting and the shattering
    of the sea.

As I sat musing, 'twas a host in dark array,
With their horses and their cannon wheeling onward
    to the fray,   10
Moving like a shadow to the fate the brave must dree,
And behind me roared the drums, rang the trumpets
    of the sea.

WALTER DE LA MARE
(*20th Century*)

1. As " I " sat musing what did " I " really see ?

2. What things in the poem led you to answer the above
   question as you did ?

3. Read the poem omitting the last line in each stanza. How
   does this help you to answer the above two questions ?

4. Why does line 12 affect us so much more than line 8 ?

Notes : page 237.

THE ICE-CART

Perched on my city office-stool
I watched with envy while a cool
And lucky carter handled ice . . .

And I was wandering in a trice
Far from the grey and grimy heat
Of that intolerable street
O'er sapphire berg and emerald floe
Beneath the still cold ruby glow
Of everlasting Polar night,
Bewildered by the queer half-light,
Until I stumbled unawares
Upon a creek where big white bears
Plunged headlong down with flourished heels
And floundered after shining seals
Through shivering seas of blinding blue.
And, as I watched them, ere I knew
I'd stripped and I was swimming too
Among the seal-pack, young and hale,
And thrusting on with threshing tail,
With twist and twirl and sudden leap
Through crackling ice and salty deep—
Diving and doubling with my kind
Until at last we left behind
Those big white blundering bulks of death,
And lay at length with panting breath
Upon a far untravelled floe
Beneath a gentle drift of snow—
Snow drifting gently fine and white
Out of the endless Polar night,

Falling and falling evermore   30
Upon that far untravelled shore
Till I was buried fathoms deep
Beneath that cold white drifting sleep—
Sleep drifting deep,
Deep drifting sleep . . .   35

The carter cracked a sudden whip :
I clutched my stool with startled grip,
Awakening to the grimy heat
Of that intolerable street.

WILFRID WILSON GIBSON
(*20th Century*)

1. How far is the dream picture a contrast to the actual surroundings ?

2. Point out some of the most effective uses of alliteration in the poem.

3. Why does the poet at the end bring us back to

    The grimy heat
    Of that intolerable street ?

Notes : page 238.

OLD GREY SQUIRREL

A great while ago, there was a school-boy.
   He lived in a cottage by the sea.
And the very first thing he could remember
   Was the rigging of the schooners by the quay.

He could watch them, when he woke, from his
     window,   5
   With the tall cranes hoisting out the freight.
And he used to think of shipping as a sea-cook,
   And sailing to the Golden Gate.

For he used to buy the yellow penny-dreadfuls,
   And read them where he fished for conger-eels,   10
And listened to the lapping of the water,
   The green and oily water round the keels.

There were trawlers with their shark-mouthed flat-
     fish,
   And red nets hanging out to dry,
And the skate the skipper kept because he liked 'em,   15
   And landsmen never knew the fish to fry.

There were brigantines with timber out of Norroway,
   Oozing with the syrups of the pine.
There were rusty dusty schooners out of Sunderland,
   And ships of the Blue Cross line.   20

And to tumble down a hatch into the cabin
   Was better than the best of broken rules ;
For the smell of 'em was like a Christmas dinner,
   And the feel of 'em was like a box of tools.

And, before he went to sleep in the evening,   25
   The very last thing that he could see
Was the sailor men a-dancing in the moonlight
   By the capstan that stood upon the quay.

He is perched upon a high stool in London.
  The Golden Gate is very far away.   30
They caught him, and they caged him like a squirrel.
  He is totting up accounts, and going grey.

He will never, never, never sail to 'Frisco.
  But the very last thing that he will see
Will be sailor-men a-dancing in the sunrise   35
  By the capstan that stands upon the quay . . .

To the tune of an old concertina,
  By the capstan that stands upon the quay.

ALFRED NOYES

(*20th Century*)

1. Half the charm of this poem lies in its rhythm. It cannot
   be felt unless it is read aloud.

2. What gives the peculiar rippling effect to this rhythm ?

3. In reading the poem aloud I slow down the rhythm in
   certain places. Do you ?

4. Is the poem sad ?

5. Compare this poem with the next.

Notes : page 239.

SIMON DANZ

(A DUTCH PICTURE)

Simon Danz has come home again
  From cruising about with his buccaneers;
He has singed the beard of the King of Spain,
And carried away the Dean of Jaen
  And sold him in Algiers.   5

In his house by the Maese, with its roof of tiles
  And weathercocks flying aloft in air,
There are silver tankards of antique styles,
Plunder of convent and castle, and piles
  Of carpets rich and rare.   10

In his tulip-garden there by the town,
  Overlooking the sluggish stream,
With his Moorish cap and dressing-gown,
The old sea-captain, hale and brown,
  Walks in a waking dream.   15

A smile in his gray mustachio lurks
  Whenever he thinks of the King of Spain,
And the listed tulips look like Turks,
And the silent gardener as he works
  Is changed to the Dean of Jaen.   20

The windmills on the outermost verge
  Of the landscape in the haze
To him are towns on the Spanish coast,
With whiskered sentinels at their post,
  Though this is the River Maese.   25

But when the winter rains begin,
  He sits and smokes by the blazing brands,
And old seafaring men come in,
Goat-bearded, grey, and with double chin,
  And rings upon their hands.   30

They sit there in the shadow and shine
  Of the flickering fire of the winter night ;
Figures in colour and design
Like those by Rembrandt of the Rhine,
  Half darkness and half light,   35

And they talk of ventures lost or won,
  And their talk is ever and ever the same,
While they drink the red wine of Tarragon,
From the cellars of some Spanish don
  Or convent set on flame.   40

Restless at times, with heavy strides
  He paces his parlour to and fro ;
He is like a ship that at anchor rides
And swings with the rising and falling tides,
  And tugs at her anchor-tow.   45

Voices mysterious far and near,
  Sound of the wind and sound of the sea,
Are calling and whispering in his ear :
" Simon Danz ! Why stayest thou here ?
  Come forth and follow me ! "   50

So he thinks he shall take to the sea again
  For one more cruise with his buccaneers,
To singe the beard of the King of Spain,
And capture another Dean of Jaen
  And sell him in Algiers.   55

LONGFELLOW
(1807-1882)

1. Compare this poem with " Old Grey Squirrel ".

2. This poem divides up naturally into four parts, an
   introduction and three pictures. Why is there no
   conclusion ?

3. Which picture do you prefer ?

4. Which stanza gives best the atmosphere of the poem ?

5. Lines 51-55. Do you think Simon Danz took to the sea
   again ?

   Notes : page 240.

71

THE TOLL-GATE HOUSE

The toll-gate's gone, but still stands lone,
In the dip of the hill, the horse of stone,
And over the roof in the branching pine
The great owl sits in the white moonshine.
An old man lives, and lonely, there,   5
His windows yet on the cross-roads stare,
And on Michaelmas night in all the years
A galloping far and faint he hears . . .
His casement open wide he flings
With " Who goes there ? " and a lantern swings . . .   10
But never more in the dim moonbeam
Than a cloak and a plume and the silver gleam
Of passing spurs in the night can he see,
For the toll-gate's gone, and the road is free.

JOHN DRINKWATER
(*20th Century*)

1. (*a*) In how many ways does the poet tell us of the loneliness of the spot ?

   (*b*) Why is he so anxious to emphasise this ?

2. How far is the story true ?

3. What effect has the last line on our belief in the story ?

   Notes : page 241.

THE WAY THROUGH THE WOODS

They shut the road through the woods
Seventy years ago.
Weather and rain have undone it again,
And now you would never know
There was once a road through the woods   5
Before they planted the trees.
It is underneath the coppice and heath,
And the thin anemones.
Only the keeper sees
That, where the ring-dove broods,   10
And the badgers roll at ease,
There was once a road through the woods.

Yet, if you enter the woods
Of a summer evening late,
When the night-air cools on the trout-ringed pools   15
Where the otter whistles his mate
(They fear not men in the woods,
Because they see so few)
You will hear the beat of a horse's feet,
And the swish of a skirt in the dew,   20
Steadily cantering through
The misty solitudes,
As though they perfectly knew
The old lost road through the woods . . .
But there is no road through the woods!   25

RUDYARD KIPLING
(1865-1936)

1. How often are we told in the first stanza that there is no
   road through the woods?
2. Why is the poet so anxious to emphasise this?
3. Line 13. What is the effect of the word " yet " ?
4. Where do you feel the effect of the rhythm most in the
   poem?
5. Which poem is the more convincing, this one, or " The Toll-
   gate House " ?
6. What effect has the last line on our belief in this story?

   Notes : page 241.

FLANNAN ISLE

Though three men dwell on Flannan Isle
To keep the lamp alight,
As we steered under the lee we caught
No glimmer through the night.

A passing ship at dawn had brought   5
The news, and quickly we set sail
To find out what strange thing might ail
The keepers of the deep-sea light.

The winter day broke blue and bright
With glancing sun and glancing spray   10
While o'er the swell our boat made way,
As gallant as a gull in flight.

But as we neared the lonely Isle
And looked up at the naked height,
And saw the lighthouse towering white   15
With blinded lantern that all night
Had never shot a spark
Of comfort through the dark,
So ghostly in the cold sunlight
It seemed that we were struck the while   20
With wonder all too dread for words.
And, as into the tiny creek
We stole, beneath the hanging crag
We saw three queer black ugly birds—
Too big by far in my belief   25
For cormorant or shag—
Like seamen sitting bolt-upright
Upon a half-tide reef :
But as we neared they plunged from sight
Without a sound or spirt of white.   30

And still too mazed to speak,
We landed and made fast the boat
And climbed the track in single file,
Each wishing he were safe afloat
On any sea, however far,   35
So it be far from Flannan Isle :
And still we seemed to climb and climb
As though we'd lost all count of time
And so must climb for evermore ;
Yet all too soon we reached the door—   40
The black sun-blistered lighthouse door
That gaped for us ajar.

As on the threshold for a spell
We paused, we seemed to breathe the smell
Of limewash and of tar,   45
Familiar as our daily breath,
As though 'twere some strange scent of death ;
And so yet wondering side by side
We stood a moment still tongue-tied,
And each with black foreboding eyed   50
The door ere we should fling it wide
To leave the sunlight for the gloom :
Till, plucking courage up, at last
Hard on each other's heels we passed
Into the living-room.   55

Yet as we crowded through the door
We only saw a table spread
For dinner, meat and cheese and bread,
But all untouched and no one there ;
As though when they sat down to eat,   60
Ere they could even taste,
Alarm had come and they in haste
Had risen and left the bread and meat,
For at the table-head a chair
Lay tumbled on the floor.   65

We listened, but we only heard
The feeble cheeping of a bird
That starved upon its perch;
And, listening still, without a word
We set about our hopeless search.   70
We hunted high, we hunted low,
And soon ransacked the empty house;
Then o'er the Island to and fro
We ranged, to listen and to look
In every cranny, cleft or nook   75
That might have hid a bird or mouse:
But though we searched from shore to shore
We found no sign in any place,
And soon again stood face to face
Before the gaping door,   80
And stole into the room once more
As frightened children steal.
Ay, though we hunted high and low
And hunted everywhere,
Of the three men's fate we found no trace   85
Of any kind in any place
But a door ajar and an untouched meal
And an overtoppled chair.

And as we listened in the gloom
Of that forsaken living-room—   90
A chill clutch on our breath—
We thought how ill-chance came to all
Who kept the Flannan Light,
And how the rock had been the death
Of many a likely lad—   95
How six had come to a sudden end
And three had gone stark mad,
And one, whom we'd all known as friend,
Had leapt from the lantern one still night
And fallen dead by the lighthouse wall—   100
And long we thought
On the three we sought,
And on what might yet befall.

Like curs a glance has brought to heel
We listened, flinching there,   105
And looked and looked on the untouched meal
And the overtoppled chair.

We seemed to stand for an endless while,
Though still no word was said,
Three men alive on Flannan Isle   110
Who thought on three men dead.

WILFRID WILSON GIBSON
(*20th Century*)

The Flannan Isles, or The Seven Hunters, as they are
sometimes called, are a group of small rocky islands about 15
miles W.N.W. of Gallon Head in Lewis. Imagine yourself
standing on Gallon Head on a clear sunny day. Away to
the west before you there is nothing but sea for thousands of
miles, the whole breadth of the Atlantic Ocean. As your eyes
sweep round to the W.N.W. you see a group of little islets,
15 miles away, like lonely rocks in the great sea. I remember
standing on the highest point in the island of Iona, and
looking through glasses away out to the west. There in
the sunlight like a thin white pencil on the horizon was
Skerryvore, the famous lighthouse. I cannot tell you how
lonely it looked in the great waste of waters, and how fragile,
like a child's toy. Something like this I imagine the lighthouse
on Flannan Isle would appear to you, standing on Gallon
Head.

1. Is the story true ?

2. Read lines 9-12. In what mood were the three men as
   they approached Flannan Isle ?

3. Professor Murray says, " R. L. Stevenson makes
   somewhere the interesting remark that his pirates
   in *Treasure Island* never actually use a bad word, yet
   they make the requisite blood-curdling impression.
   That is Art." Does this suggest a statement you might
   make concerning lines 1-88 of this poem ?

4. Is the story finished ?

Notes : page 242.

77

SKATING

And in the frosty season, when the sun
Was set, and visible for many a mile
The cottage windows blazed through twilight gloom,
I heeded not their summons : happy time
It was indeed for all of us—for me   5
It was a time of rapture ! Clear and loud
The village clock tolled six—I wheeled about,
Proud and exulting like an untired horse
That cares not for his home. All shod with steel,
We hissed along the polished ice in games   10
Confederate, imitative of the chase
And woodland pleasures—the resounding horn,
The pack loud chiming, and the hunted hare.
So through the darkness and the cold we flew,
And not a voice was idle ; with the din   15
Smitten, the precipices rang aloud ;
The leafless trees and every icy crag
Tinkled like iron ; while far distant hills
Into the tumult sent an alien sound
Of melancholy not unnoticed, while the stars   20
Eastward were sparkling clear, and in the west
The orange sky of evening died away.
Not seldom from the uproar I retired
Into a silent bay, or sportively
Glanced sideway, leaving the tumultuous throng,   25
To cut across the reflex of a star
That fled, and, flying still before me, gleamed
Upon the glassy plain ; and oftentimes,
When we had given our bodies to the wind,
And all the shadowy banks on either side   30

Came sweeping through the darkness, spinning still
The rapid line of motion, then at once
Have I, reclining back upon my heels,
Stopped short ; yet still the solitary cliffs
Wheeled by me —even as if the earth had rolled
With visible motion her diurnal round !
Behind me did they stretch in solemn train,
Feebler and feebler, and I stood and watched
Till all was tranquil as a dreamless sleep.

(" The Prelude ", *Book I, lines* 425-463)

35

WORDSWORTH

(1770-1850)

In this passage Wordsworth describes scenes from his boyhood. The cottage windows (line 3) are in Hawkshead, close to the shores of Esthwaite, the lake on which the boys were skating.

As a boy he evidently

(*a*) saw clearly,
(*b*) felt deeply,
(*c*) was sensitive to the appeal of nature.

Can you prove this from the passage ?

Notes : page 244.

THE BOY AND THE OWLS

There was a Boy : ye knew him well, ye cliffs
And islands of Winander !—many a time
At evening, when the earliest stars began
To move along the edges of the hills,
Rising or setting, would he stand alone   5
Beneath the trees or by the glimmering lake,
And there, with fingers interwoven, both hands
Pressed closely palm to palm, and to his mouth
Uplifted, he, as through an instrument,
Blew mimic hootings to the silent owls,   10
That they might answer him ; and they would shout
Across the watery vale, and shout again,
Responsive to his call, with quivering peals,
And long halloos and screams, and echoes loud,
Redoubled and redoubled, concourse wild   15
Of jocund din ; and, when a lengthened pause
Of silence came and baffled his best skill,
Then sometimes, in that silence while he hung
Listening, a gentle shock of mild surprise
Has carried far into his heart the voice   20
Of mountain torrents ; or the visible scene
Would enter unawares into his mind,
With all its solemn imagery, its rocks,
Its woods, and that uncertain heaven, received
Into the bosom of the steady lake.   25

("The Prelude ", *Book V, lines* 364-388)

WORDSWORTH
(1770-1850)

1. As you see, this is part of the same poem as "Skating".
   Do you see any resemblance between this boy and the
   boy, William Wordsworth, in "Skating"?

2. Which of these two boys really had the experience given
   in lines 16-24 ?

Notes : page 244.

THE HAWK

The hawk slipt out of the pine, and rose in the sunlit
    air :
Steady and still he poised ; his shadow slept on the
    grass :
And the bird's song sickened and sank : she cowered
    with furtive stare
Dumb, till the quivering dimness should flicker and
    shift and pass.

Suddenly down he dropped : she heard the hiss of
    his wing,
Fled with a scream of terror : oh, would she had
    dared to rest !
For the hawk at eve was full, and there was no bird to
    sing,
And over the heather drifted the down from a bleeding
    breast.

A. C. BENSON
(20th Century)

Read now "The Buzzards", page 82.

1. What is the first thing in this poem that makes you
think of "The Buzzards" ?

2. Why are your feelings towards the hawk different from
those towards the buzzards ?

3. Which line do you like best ?

Notes : page 245.

THE BUZZARDS

When evening came and the warm glow grew deeper
And every tree that bordered the green meadows
And in the yellow cornfields every reaper
And every corn-shock stood above their shadows
Flung eastward from their feet in longer measure,   5
Serenely far there swam in the sunny height
A buzzard and his mate who took their pleasure
Swirling and poising idly in golden light.

On great pied motionless moth-wings borne along,
  So effortless and so strong,   10
Cutting each other's paths, together they glided,
Then wheeled asunder till they soared divided
Two valleys' width (as though it were delight
To part like this, being sure they could unite
So swiftly in their empty, free dominion)   15
Curved headlong downward, towered up the sunny
    steep,
Then, with a sudden lift of the one great pinion,
Swung proudly to a curve and from its height
Took half a mile of sunlight in one long sweep.

And we, so small on the swift immense hillside,   20
Stood tranced, until our souls arose uplifted
  On those far-sweeping, wide,
Strong curves of flight—swayed up and hugely drifted,
Were washed, made strong and beautiful in the tide
Of sun-bathed air. But far beneath, beholden   25
Through shining deeps of air, the fields were golden
And rosy burned the heather where cornfields ended.

And still those buzzards wheeled, while light withdrew
Out of the vales and to surging slopes ascended,
Till the loftiest-flaming summit died to blue.   30

MARTIN ARMSTRONG
(*20th Century*)

How beautiful the flight of the buzzard in the sunlight can
be I only realised lately. I was standing alone on Cara Head
(Cara is a little uninhabited island off the coast of Kintyre). It
was a perfect July day. The immense sweep of blue sky above
and blue sea below, Jura, Islay, the coast of Kintyre
stretching away to the Mull, and the coast of Ireland in the
distance—all combined to make a picture not easily forgotten.
I rounded a big rock and startled a buzzard which was resting
there. It sailed out over the cliffs and then rose in wide
sweeping circles, with never a flap of the wing as far as I
could see, up and up—

> *On great pied motionless moth-wings borne along,*
> *So effortless and so strong,*

until, when I glanced aside for a moment, I could not
find it again. In my picture there were only the bird and
the sunlight. Everything else was forgotten.

Here now is the poem with about half the lines omitted :

> When evening came and the warm glow grew deeper,
> Serenely far there swam in the sunny height
> A buzzard and his mate who took their pleasure
> Swirling and poising idly in golden light.
> On great pied motionless moth-wings borne along,
>   So effortless and so strong,
> Cutting each other's paths, together they glided,
> Then wheeled asunder till they soared divided
> Two valleys' width,
> Curved headlong downward, towered up the sunny
>   steep,
> Then, with a sudden lift of the one great pinion,
> Swung proudly to a curve, and from its height
> Took half a mile of sunlight in one long sweep.
> And still those buzzards wheeled, while light withdrew
> Out of the vales and to surging slopes ascended,
> Till the loftiest-flaming summit died to blue.

In this picture, too, there are only the birds and the sunlight.
Everything else has been omitted. Have we lost anything of
importance ?

Notes : page 245.

THE LARK'S SONG

In Mercer Street the light slants down,
And straightway an enchanted town
Is round him, pinnacle and spire
Flash back, elate, the sudden fire;
And clear above the silent street
Falls suddenly and strangely sweet 5
The lark's song. Bubbling, note on note
Rise fountain-like, o'erflow and float
Tide upon tide, and make more fair
The magic of the sunlit air. 10
No more the cage can do him wrong,
All is forgotten save his song;
He has forgot the ways of men,
Wide heaven is over him again,
And round him the wide fields of dew 15
That his first infant mornings knew,
Ere yet the dolorous years had brought
The hours of captive anguish, fraught
With the vile clamour of the street,
The insult of the passing feet, 20
The torture of the daily round,
The organ's blasphemy of sound.
Sudden some old swift memory brings
The knowledge of forgotten wings,
He springs elate and panting falls 25
At the rude touch of prison walls.
Silence. Again the street is grey;
Shut down the windows. Work-a-day.

From " In Mercer Street "

Seumas O'Sullivan
(*20th Century*)

1. Lines 1-10.   A most beautiful picture.   This is the same
   Mercer Street as that of " A Piper ".
   (Book III, page 65).

   What is the street usually like ?

2. Lines 1-4.   Which is the most effective word in these lines,
   effective from a certain peculiarity in its use ?

3. Lines 5-10.   A wonderful description of the bird's song.

4. What do you think of the last two lines ?

5. Is the bird the only captive ?

6. Compare this poem with " Reverie of Poor Susan "
   (Book III, page 75).   Note that Wordsworth also refers
   to the lark's song as " a note of enchantment ".

Notes : page 246.

THE HOUSE BEAUTIFUL

A naked house, a naked moor,
A shivering pool before the door,
A garden bare of flowers and fruit
And poplars at the garden foot:
Such is the place that I live in,   5
Bleak without and bare within.

Yet shall your ragged moor receive
The incomparable pomp of eve,
And the cold glories of the dawn
Behind your shivering trees be drawn ;   10
And when the wind from place to place
Doth the unmoored cloud-galleons chase,
Your garden gloom and gleam again,
With leaping sun, with glancing rain.
Here shall the wizard moon ascend   15
The heavens, in the crimson end
Of day's declining splendour ; here
The army of the stars appear.
The neighbour hollows dry or wet,
Spring shall with tender flowers beset ;   20
And oft the morning muser see
Larks rising from the broomy lea,
And every fairy wheel and thread
Of cobweb dew-bediamonded.
When daisies go, shall winter time   25
Silver the simple grass with rime ;
Autumnal frosts enchant the pool
And make the cart-ruts beautiful ;
And when snow-bright the moor expands,
How shall your children clap their hands !   30

To make this earth our hermitage,
A cheerful and a changeful page,
God's bright and intricate device
Of days and seasons doth suffice.

R. L. STEVENSON
(1850-1894)

1. Lines 1-6. We are so inclined to associate ugliness and dullness with the town, that these lines remind us that others can find the country just as dull.

Line 4. Why poplars ? Would elm-trees do as well ?

2. Lines 7-10. There are two words in these lines which seem to us to be wonderfully effective. Can you find them ?

3. Lines 13-14. Note the alliteration.

Here we have " glancing " rain, and in " To S. R. Crockett " (page 163, line 1) " flying " rain. How different from " And the rain dropped " of " The Common Street " ! (Page 88).

4. Line 15. Why " wizard " ?

5. Line 18. Why is this line specially appropriate ?

6. Lines 31-34. What do you think of these four lines ?

Notes : page 248.

THE COMMON STREET

The common street climbed up against the sky,
Grey meeting grey ; and wearily to and fro
I saw the patient, common people go,
Each with his sordid burden trudging by.

And the rain dropped ; there was not any sigh   5
Or stir of a live wind ; dull, dull, and slow
All motion ; as a tale told long ago
The faded world ; and creeping night drew nigh.

Then burst the sunset, flooding far and fleet,
Leavening the whole of life with magic leaven.   10
Suddenly down the long, wet glistening hill

Pure splendour poured—and lo ! the common street,
A golden highway into golden heaven,
With the dark shapes of men ascending still.

HELEN GRAY CONE
(20th Century)

1. **Lines** 1-8. Note how many words and phrases here
   emphasise the dull lifelessness of the **street**.

2. Line 4. Why " sordid " burden ?

3. Lines 1-8. This is a picture in grey, and dull **grey at that**.
   There is no contrast—"Grey meeting grey". In what
   colours would you paint the second picture, lines 9-14 ?

4. Line 9. Why " burst " ?

5. From the indications in the **poem** can you tell in what
   direction the street rises, *i.e.*, whether it rises towards the
   North or South, etc. ? Has this any definite effect upon
   the picture ?

6. What has the poetess omitted in the last line ? Was she
   right to omit it ?

Notes : page 248.

THE KNIGHT'S TOMB

Where is the grave of Sir Arthur O'Kellyn?
Where may the grave of that good man be?—
By the side of a spring, on the breast of Helvellyn,
Under the twigs of a young birch tree !
The oak that in summer was sweet to hear,   5
And rustled its leaves in the fall of the year,
And whistled and roared in the winter alone,
Is gone, and the birch in its stead is grown.
The Knight's bones are dust,
And his good sword rust :   10
His soul is with the saints, I trust.

COLERIDGE
(1772-1834)

1. Is this a sad poem ?

2. How would you read it ?

3. What is its atmosphere ?

   Notes : page 249.

THE DEAD KNIGHT

The cleanly rush of the mountain air,
And the mumbling, grumbling humble-bees,
Are the only things that wander there,
The pitiful bones are laid at ease,
The grass has grown in his tangled hair,   5
And a rambling bramble binds his knees.

To shrieve his soul from the pangs of hell,
The only requiem-bells that rang
Were the hare-bell and the heather-bell:
Hushed he is with the holy spell   10
In the gentle hymn the wind sang,
And he lies quiet, and sleeps well.

He is bleached and blanched with the summer sun;
The misty rain and the cold dew
Have altered him from the kingly one   15
(That his lady loved, and his men knew)
And dwindled him to a skeleton.

The vetches have twined about his bones,
The straggling ivy twists and creeps
In his eye-sockets; the nettle keeps   20
Vigil about him while he sleeps.
Over his body the wind moans
With a dreary tune throughout the day,
In a chorus wistful, eerie, thin
As the gull's cry—as the cry in the bay,   25
The mournful word the seas say
When tides are wandering out or in.

JOHN MASEFIELD
(20*th Century*)

1. Describe the knight's resting-place.

2. Is this a sad poem?

3. Compare the atmosphere of this poem with that of the last.

Notes : page 250

THE TWA CORBIES

As I was walking all alane,
I heard twa corbies making a mane:
The tane unto the tither say,
" Whar sall we gang and dine the day? "

" In behint yon auld fail dyke   5
I wot there lies a new-slain knight;
And naebody kens that he lies there
But his hawk, his hound, and his lady fair.

His hound is to the hunting gane,
His hawk to fetch the wild-fowl hame,   10
His lady's ta'en anither mate,
So we may mak our dinner sweet.

" Ye'll sit on his white hause-bane,
And I'll pike out his bonny blue e'en;
Wi' ae lock o' his gowden hair   15
We'll theek our nest when it grows bare.

" Mony a one for him maks mane,
But nane sall ken whar he is gane;
O'er his white banes, when they are bare,
The wind sall blaw for evermair ".   20

ANONYMOUS

tane : *one*	hause : *neck*
tither : *other*	theek : *thatch*
corbies : *ravens*	mane : *moan*
fail dyke : *wall of turf*	

1. Is this a sad poem?

2. Some people object to this poem and say it is too
   gruesome. Do you agree with this?

Notes : page 250.

FEAR NO MORE THE HEAT O' THE SUN

Guiderius and Arviragus, the sons of Cymbeline, King of Britain, were stolen away while still very young and brought up to manhood among the Welsh mountains by Belarius. Some twenty years later, Imogen, the daughter of Cymbeline, fled from her father's court to Milford Haven in the disguise of a young man, adopting the name Fidele. She lost her way and by chance arrived at the cave in which her brothers dwelt. Thinking her a boy, they welcomed their sister, whom they had never seen, and both were strangely drawn to her.

> " And at first meeting loved,
> Continued so, until we thought he died."

Next morning, feeling ill, she remained in the cave while they went out to hunt. She took a drug, trusting it would revive her, but, instead, it cast her into a death-like sleep. When they returned, Arviragus went to the cave to call her. He did not return at once and the others were blaming him, when

Re-enter Arviragus *with* Imogen, *as dead,*
bearing her in his arms.

Bel. :   Look, here he comes,
And brings the dire occasion in his arms
Of what we blame him for !

Arv. :   The bird is dead
That we have made so much on. I had rather
Have skipp'd from sixteen years of age to sixty,
To have turn'd my leaping-time into a crutch,
Than have seen this.

Gui. :   O sweetest, fairest lily !
My brother wears thee not the one half so well
As when thou grew'st thyself. . . .

Bel. : How found you him?

Arv. :   Stark, as you see :
Thus smiling, as some fly had tickled slumber,
Not as death's dart, being laugh'd at ; his right cheek
Reposing on a cushion

Gui. :   Where?

Arv. :   O' the floor ;
His arms thus leagued : I thought he slept, and put
My clouted brogues from off my feet, whose rudeness
Answer'd my steps too loud.

Gui. :   Why, he but sleeps :
If he be gone, he'll make his grave a bed :
With female fairies will his tomb be haunted,
And worms will not come to thee.   .   .   .
                                Let us bury him
And not protract with admiration what
Is now due debt. To the grave.   .   .   .

Arv. :   Be't so :
And let us . . . though now our voices
Have got the mannish crack, sing him to the
ground. . . .

Gui. : I cannot sing : I'll weep, and word it with thee ;
For notes of sorrow out of tune are worse
Than priests and fanes that lie.

Arv. :   We'll speak it, then. . .
     Brother, begin. . . .

Song

Gui. : Fear no more the heat o' the sun,
    Nor the furious winter's rages ;
Thou thy worldly task hast done,
    Home art gone, and ta'en thy wages :   5
Golden lads and girls all must,
As chimney-sweepers, come to dust.

Arv. : Fear no more the frown o' the great,
    Thou art past the tyrant's stroke ;
Care no more to clothe and eat ;
    To thee the reed is as the oak :   10
The sceptre, learning, physic, must
All follow this, and come to dust.

Gui. : Fear no more the lightning-flash,
Arv. :   Nor the all-dreaded thunder-stone ;
Gui. : Fear nor slander, censure rash ;
Arv. :   Thou hast finish'd joy and moan :   15
Both : All lovers young, all lovers must
    Consign to thee, and come to dust.

Gui. : No exorciser harm thee !
Arv. : Nor no witchcraft charm thee !   20
Gui. : Ghost unlaid forbear thee !
Arv. : Nothing ill come near thee !
Both : Quiet consummation have ;
    And renownéd be thy grave !

"Cymbeline", *Act IV, Sc. I*

SHAKESPEARE
(1564-1616)

censure : *judgment*   exorciser : *magician*

The following questions refer only to the song :

1. How does the atmosphere of this poem differ from that
   of the last ?
2. To what things in the poem is this change due ?

Notes : page 251

DEATH THE LEVELLER

The glories of our blood and state
  Are shadows, not substantial things;
There is no armour against fate;
  Death lays his icy hand on kings:
     Sceptre and Crown   5
     Must tumble down,
And in the dust be equal made
With the poor crooked scythe and spade.

Some men with swords may reap the field,
  And plant fresh laurels where they kill: 10
But their strong nerves at last must yield;
  They tame but one another still:
     Early or late
     They stoop to fate,
And must give up their murmuring breath   15
When they, pale captives, creep to death.

The garlands wither on your brow;
  Then boast no more your mighty deeds;
Upon Death's purple altar now
  See where the victor-victim bleeds: 20
     Your heads must come
     To the cold tomb;
Only the actions of the just
Smell sweet, and blossom in their dust.

SHIRLEY
(1596-1666)

1. We might summarise part of the last poem in the sentence,
   " All must come to dust ". Would those words serve as
   a summary of this poem?

2. Choose six lines (not necessarily coming together) from
   this poem which sum up the main thoughts in it.

3. In what way does the atmosphere of this poem differ from
   that of the last?

4. To what is this change of atmosphere chiefly due?
   Notes : page 252.

OZYMANDIAS

I met a traveller from an antique land
Who said : Two vast and trunkless legs of stone
Stand in the desert. Near them, on the sand,
Half sunk, a shattered visage lies, whose frown,
And wrinkled lip, and sneer of cold command   5
Tell that its sculptor well those passions read
Which yet survive, stamped on these lifeless things,
The hand that mocked them and the heart that fed :

And on the pedestal these words appear :
" My name is Ozymandias, king of kings :   10
Look on my works, ye Mighty, and despair ! "
Nothing beside remains. Round the decay
Of that colossal wreck, boundless and bare
The lone and level sands stretch far away.

SHELLEY
(1792-1822)

1. This poem might be considered as an example or illustration
   of the teaching of the last poem. But the atmosphere
   of the two poems is quite different. What makes the
   difference ?

2. Are any indications given of the character of Ozymandias ?

3. From the point of view of grammar, lines 3-8 form a very
   complex sentence, but it is so well constructed that its
   meaning should be quite clear.

4. What does Shelley mean by " The hand that *mocked*
   them " ?

5. Lines 12-14. Perhaps the finest picture in literature of the
   bareness and infinite stretch of the desert. How is the
   effect produced ?

Notes : page 252.

EGYPT'S MIGHT IS TUMBLED DOWN

Egypt's might is tumbled down
  Down a-down the deeps of thought;
Greece is fallen and Troy town,
Glorious Rome hath lost her crown,
  Venice' pride is nought.   5

But the dreams their children dreamed
  Fleeting, unsubstantial, vain,
Shadowy as the shadows seemed,
Airy nothing, as they deemed,
  These remain.   10

MARY COLERIDGE
(1861-1907)

1. What have we lost if we turn lines 1 and 2 into " Egypt's might is tumbled down the deeps of thought " ?

2. Line 2. Why " the deeps of *thought* " ?

3. Stanza 2. (*a*) Of which poem in the earlier part of this book does the stanza remind you ?
    (*b*) To whom does line 6 refer ?

4. Line 10. If we change this line to " These alone remain ", what do we gain or lose ?

5. Compare this poem with the last. What has become of the dream of Ozymandias ? Why ?

As a companion picture to stanza 1 above, take stanza XVIII of " The Rubaiyat of Omar Khayyám " :

They say the Lion and the Lizard keep
The Courts where Jamshyd gloried and drank deep ;
And Bahram, that great Hunter—the Wild Ass
Stamps o'er his Head, but cannot break his Sleep.

Notes : page 253

WHERE ROSE THE MOUNTAINS

Where rose the mountains, there to him were friends;
Where roll'd the ocean, thereon was his home;
Where a blue sky, and glowing clime, extends,
He had the passion and the power to roam;
The desert, forest, cavern, breaker's foam,   5
Were unto him companionship; they spake
A mutual language, clearer than the tome
Of his land's tongue, which he would oft forsake
For Nature's pages glass'd by sunbeams on the lake.

But in Man's dwellings he became a thing   10
Restless and worn, and stern and wearisome,
Droop'd as a wild-born falcon with clipt wing,
To whom the boundless air alone were home:
Then came his fit again, which to o'ercome,
As eagerly the barr'd-up bird will beat   15
His breast and beak against his wiry dome
Till the blood tinge his plumage, so the heat
Of his impeded soul would through his bosom eat.

("Childe Harold's Pilgrimage", Canto III, Stanzas XIII, XV.)

BYRON
(1788-1824)

1. "Childe" is an old word for "Knight", so that Childe
   Harold in modern English would be Sir Harold. As
   Childe Harold is just Byron himself, though here he speaks
   of him in the third person, you should be able to form
   some idea of the character of the poet from the above
   two stanzas.

2. Stanza 2, line 1. Which is the most expressive word in
   this line?

3. Which is the most beautiful picture and the most powerful
   line in the above stanzas?

4. In what way does the pride of Byron differ from that of
   Ozymandias?

   Notes: page 254.

THE OCEAN

There is a pleasure in the pathless woods,
There is a rapture on the lonely shore,
There is society, where none intrudes,
By the deep Sea, and music in its roar:
I love not Man the less, but Nature more,   5
From these our interviews, in which I steal
From all I may be, or have been before,
To mingle with the Universe, and feel
What I can ne'er express, yet cannot all conceal.

Roll on, thou deep and dark blue Ocean—roll!   10
Ten thousand fleets sweep over thee in vain;
Man marks the earth with ruin—his control
Stops with the shore; upon the watery plain
The wrecks are all thy deed, nor doth remain
A shadow of man's ravage, save his own,   15
When, for a moment, like a drop of rain,
He sinks into thy depths with bubbling groan
Without a grave, unknell'd, uncoffin'd and unknown.

His steps are not upon thy paths—thy fields
Are not a spoil for him—thou dost arise   20
And shake him from thee; the vile strength he wields
For earth's destruction thou dost all despise,
Spurning him from thy bosom to the skies,
And send'st him, shivering in thy playful spray
And howling, to his Gods, where haply lies   25
His petty hope in some near port or bay,
And dashest him again to earth:—there let him lay.

The armaments which thunderstrike the walls
Of rock-built cities, bidding nations quake,
And monarchs tremble in their capitals,   30
The oak leviathans, whose huge ribs make
Their clay creator the vain title take
Of lord of thee, and arbiter of war—
These are thy toys, and, as the snowy flake,
They melt into thy yeast of waves, which mar   35
Alike the Armada's pride or spoils of Trafalgar.

Thy shores are empires, changed in all save thee—
Assyria, Greece, Rome, Carthage, what are they?
Thy waters wash'd them power while they were free,
And many a tyrant since; their shores obey   40
The stranger, slave, or savage; their decay
Has dried up realms to deserts :—not so thou—
Unchangeable save to thy wild waves' play,
Time writes no wrinkle on thine azure brow—
Such as creation's dawn beheld, thou rollest now.   45

Thou glorious mirror, where the Almighty's form
Glasses itself in tempests; in all time,
Calm or convulsed—in breeze, or gale, or storm,
Icing the pole, or in the torrid clime
Dark-heaving—boundless, endless, and sublime,   50
The image of Eternity, the throne
Of the Invisible; even from out thy slime
The monsters of the deep are made; each zone
Obeys thee; thou goest forth, dread, fathomless, alone.

And I have loved thee, Ocean! and my joy   55
Of youthful sports was on thy breast to be
Borne, like thy bubbles, onward; from a boy
I wanton'd with thy breakers—they to me
Were a delight; and if the freshening sea
Made them a terror—'twas a pleasing fear,   60
For I was as it were a child of thee,
And trusted to thy billows far and near,
And laid my hand upon thy mane—as I do here.

(" Childe Harold's Pilgrimage ",
Canto IV, Stanzas CLXXVIII-CLXXXIV)

BYRON
(1788-1824)

1. Compare stanza 1 with stanza 1 of the preceding poem,
   and both with " The Seagull " (page 22).

2. Stanza 1, lines 8-9.   What do you think these lines mean ?

3. Stanzas 2-4.   What is Byron trying to show us here ?

4. Stanza 3, line 27.   Why " lay " ?

5. Stanza 5. (*a*) What is Byron trying to show us here ?
            (*b*) Quote the lines which show this most clearly.

6. Compare stanza 5 with " Egypt's Might is tumbled down "
   (page 97).

7. Stanza 6.   What is Byron trying to show us here ?

8. Our feeling of the greatness of the sea is much stronger
   in stanzas 5-6 than in stanzas 2-4.   Why ?

9. Stanza 7.   Our feeling of the greatness of the sea is
   distinctly less here than in any other stanza.   Is this
   an anticlimax ?

Notes : page 255.

TO GREECE

Clime of the unforgotten brave!
Whose land from plain to mountain-cave
Was Freedom's home, or Glory's grave!
Shrine of the mighty! can it be
That this is all remains of thee?   5
Approach, thou craven crouching slave:
    Say, is not this Thermopylae?
These waters blue that round you lave,
    O servile offspring of the free—
Pronounce what sea, what shore is this?   10
The gulf, the rock of Salamis!
These scenes, their story not unknown,
Arise, and make again your own;
Snatch from the ashes of your sires
The embers of their former fires;   15
And he who in the strife expires
Will add to theirs a name of fear,
That Tyranny shall quake to hear,
And leave his sons a hope, a fame,
They too will rather die than shame;   20
For Freedom's battle once begun,
Bequeathed by bleeding Sire to Son,
Though baffled oft is ever won.

("The Giaour")
BYRON
(1788-1824)

1. **When Byron wrote, Greece had been for over three** hundred years under the dominion of the Turks. He died while taking part in the war for the freedom of Greece.

2. Line 4. What difference would it make if "shrine" were changed to "grave"?

3. In this passage where do you feel most the passion and the power of Byron?

4. The rhyme scheme is very irregular. In one place it seems to me to weaken the effect of the lines and in one place to produce a superb effect.

Notes: page 256.

THOUGHT OF A BRITON ON THE SUBJUGATION OF SWITZERLAND

Two Voices are there; one is of the sea,
One of the mountains; each a mighty Voice:
In both from age to age thou didst rejoice,
They were thy chosen music, Liberty!
There came a Tyrant, and with holy glee   5
Thou fought'st against him; but hast vainly striven:
Thou from thy Alpine holds at length art driven,
Where not a torrent murmurs heard by thee.

Of one deep bliss thine ear hath been bereft:
Then cleave, O cleave to that which still is left;   10
For, high-souled Maid, what sorrow would it be
That Mountain floods should thunder as before,
And Ocean bellow from his rocky shore,
And neither awful Voice be heard by thee!

WORDSWORTH
(1770-1850)

1. Line 5. The tyrant is Napoleon. In 1807, when this sonnet was written, he was virtually master of the Continent of Europe.

2. Byron in the extracts from " Childe Harold " (pages 98-101) also treats of the mountains and the sea, but from a different point of view. Which point of view appeals more to you?

3. Shelley speaks of Byron's incomparable passion and power. Would you say the same of Wordsworth?

4. Suggest another name for Wordsworth's poem.

5. Lines 1 and 2. The mountains are those of Switzerland. When he refers to the sea, does he mean the sea in general or a particular sea?

Notes: page 257.

BREATHES THERE THE MAN

Breathes there the man, with soul so dead,
Who never to himself hath said,
    " This is my own, my native land ! "
Whose heart hath ne'er within him burn'd,
As home his footsteps he hath turn'd,   5
    From wandering on a foreign strand ?
If such there breathe, go, mark him well ;
For him no Minstrel raptures swell ;
High though his titles, proud his name,
Boundless his wealth as wish can claim ;   10
Despite those titles, power, and pelf,
The wretch, concentred all in self,
Living, shall forfeit fair renown,
And, doubly dying, shall go down
To the vile dust, from whence he sprung,   15
Unwept, unhonour'd, and unsung.

O Caledonia ! stern and wild,
Meet nurse for a poetic child !
Land of brown heath and shaggy wood,
Land of the mountain and the flood,   20
Land of my sires ! what mortal hand
Can e'er untie the filial band,
That knits me to thy rugged strand !

    (" The Lay of the Last Minstrel ", *Canto VI, Stanzas I, II*)

SCOTT

(1771-1832)

1. Can you form any idea of Scott from this passage ?

2. Which does this resemble more, Byron's work, or
Wordsworth's ?

3. Which lines in the poem would appeal to an Englishman,
and which would appeal most to a Scotsman ?

Notes : page 257

HE FELL AMONG THIEVES

" Ye have robbed," said he, " ye have slaughtered and
    made an end,
  Take your ill-got plunder, and bury the dead :
What will ye more of your guest and sometime
    friend ? "
  " Blood for our blood," they said.

He laughed : " If one may settle the score for five,   5
  I am ready ; but let the reckoning stand till day :
I have loved the sunlight as dearly as any alive."
  " You shall die at dawn," said they.

He flung his empty revolver down the slope,
  He climbed alone to the Eastward edge of the trees ;   10
All night long in a dream untroubled of hope
  He brooded, clasping his knees.

He did not hear the monotonous roar that fills
  The ravine where the Yassin river sullenly flows ;
He did not see the starlight on the Laspur hills,   15
  Or the far Afghan snows.

He saw the April noon on his books aglow,
  The wistaria trailing in at the window wide ;
He heard his father's voice from the terrace below
  Calling him down to ride.   20

He saw the gray little church across the park,
  The mounds that hide the loved and honoured dead ;
The Norman arch, the chancel softly dark,
  The brasses black and red.

He saw the School Close, sunny and green,   25
  The runner beside him, the stand by the parapet wall,
The distant tape, and the crowd roaring between,
  His own name over all.

He saw the dark wainscot and timbered roof,
  The long tables, and the faces merry and keen ;   30
The College Eight and their trainer dining aloof,
  The Dons on the daïs serene.

He watched the liner's stem ploughing the foam,
  He felt her trembling speed and the thrash of her
    screw ;
He heard her passengers' voices talking of home,   35
  He saw the flag she flew.

And now it was dawn. He rose strong on his feet,
  And strode to his ruined camp below the wood ;
He drank the breath of the morning cool and sweet ;
  His murderers round him stood.   40

Light on the Laspur hills was broadening fast,
  The blood-red snow-peaks chilled to a dazzling
    white :
He turned, and saw the golden circle at last,
  Cut by the Eastern height.

" O glorious Life, Who dwellest in earth and sun,   45
  I have lived, I praise and adore Thee."
                              A sword swept.
Over the pass the voices one by one
  Faded, and the hill slept.

SIR HENRY NEWBOLT
(*20th Century*)

" 'Tisn't life that matters ! 'Tis the courage you bring to it."
(" Fortitude "—Hugh Walpole)

1. Where did the poet find the title ?
2. Is the poet aiming mainly at telling a story or describing a
   character ?
3. (*a*) Is this a sad poem ?
   (*b*) What would be the effect of changing the last word in
       the poem from " slept " to " wept " ?
4. Compare Newbolt's story with that given in " Leaves from
   a Viceroy's Note-book ". For this reference I am
   indebted to the kindness of Dr. G. Pratt Insh.

Notes : page 258.

106

Outside the Agency at Gilgit, in a grove of trees, lies the grave of the first British pioneer of frontier exploration on this part of the border. This was Mr. G. W. Hayward, who, having been sent out by the Royal Geographical Society in 1868 to explore the Pamirs from Yarkand, and having failed in that direction, determined to try his fortune from another quarter, and to penetrate to the forbidden region by way of Yasin and the passes over the Hindu Kush. The story of his murder in Dakot, in July, 1870, by Mir Wali, the treacherous ruler of Yasin, acting, it is sometimes said, under the instructions of his father-in-law, Aman-ul-Mulk of Chitral, was told in his great work on Kashmir by Mr. Drew, who was at that time in the service of the Maharaja, and who recovered both the papers and the body of the murdered man. When at Dakot in August, 1885, as a member of Sir William Lockhart's Chitral mission, the late Colonel Woodthorpe met an eye-witness of the tragedy fifteen years earlier, and as this account has never yet been given to the public, it may be permissible to reproduce it here.

" It is just before dawn in the valley of Dakot. Not far from a grove of pollard willows stands a single tent, through the open door of which the light falls upon the ground in front. In this tent sits a solitary, weary man ; by his side, on the table at which he is writing, lie a rifle and a pistol, loaded. He has been warned by one whose word he cannot doubt, that Mir Wali is seeking his life that night, and he knows that from among those dark trees men are eagerly watching for a moment of unwariness on his part to rush forward across that patch of light-illumined ground and seize him. All night he has been writing to keep himself from a sleep which he knows would be fatal ; but as the first rays of dawn appear over the eternal snows, exhausted nature gives way ; his eyes close, and his head sinks—only for a moment ; but in that moment his ever-watchful and crafty enemies rush forward, and before he can seize his weapons and defend himself, he is a prisoner, and is dragged forth to death. He makes one request—it is to be allowed to ascend a low mound, and take one last glance at the earth and sky he will never look upon again. His prayer is granted ; he is unbound and as he stands up there, tall against the morning sky, with the rising sun lighting up his fair hair as a glory, he is beautiful to look upon. He glances at the sky, at those lofty snow-clad peaks and mighty glaciers reaching down into the very valley, at the valley itself, with its straggling hamlets half-hidden among the willow groves, whence rises the smoke of newly kindled fires ; he hears the noise of life beginning again, the voices of women, and the laugh of happy children, and then with firm step he comes down, back to his savage foes, and calmly says, ' I am ready.' He is instantly cut down by one of Mir Wali's men, and as he falls he receives his death-stroke from the sword of his treacherous friend, whose honoured guest he had so lately been."

Marquess Curzon
(*Leaves from a Viceroy's Note-Book*)

THE GAY GORDONS

(Dargai, October 20th, 1897)

Who's for the Gathering, who's for the Fair?
  (*Gay goes the Gordon to a fight*)
The bravest of the brave are at dead-lock there,
  (*Highlanders! march! by the right!*)
There are bullets by the hundred buzzing in the air;   5
There are bonny lads lying on the hillside bare;
But the Gordons know what the Gordons dare
  When they hear the pipers playing!

The happiest English heart to-day
  (*Gay goes the Gordon to a fight*)   10
Is the heart of the Colonel, hide it as he may
  (*Steady there! steady on the right!*)
He sees his work and he sees the way,
He knows his time and the word to say,
And he's thinking of the tune that the Gordons play 15
  When he sets the pipers playing!

Rising, roaring, rushing like the tide,
  (*Gay goes the Gordon to a fight*)
They're up through the fire-zone not to be denied;
  (*Bayonets! and charge! by the right!*)   20
Thirty bullets straight where the rest went wide,
And thirty lads are lying on the bare hillside;
But they passed in the hour of the Gordons' pride,
  To the skirl of the pipers' playing.

Sir Henry Newbolt
(*20th Century*)

Dargai is a range of hills fifty miles from Peshawar on the North-West Indian frontier. In 1897 the heights were stormed against the Afridis by the Gordon Highlanders, the 2nd Ghurkas, and the 3rd Sikhs. In the charge Piper G. Findlater was shot down, but he propped himself up against a boulder and played "The Cock o' the North", the Gordons' tune, to cheer on his comrades. For this he received the Victoria Cross.

1. The above note should make it clear why Newbolt in the
   last line of each stanza refers to the music of the pipes.
   See here Byron's reference to the pipes (page 173) and
   remember that he was George Gordon.

2. What are the Gordons doing in each stanza?

3. Stanza 3, lines 21-24. Is there anything here that reminds
   you of " He fell among Thieves "?

Notes : page 259.

ADMIRAL DEATH

Boys, are ye calling a toast to-night?
  (Hear what the sea-wind saith)
Fill for a bumper strong and bright,
  And here's to Admiral Death!
He's sailed in a hundred builds o' boat,
He's fought in a thousand kinds o' coat,
He's the senior flag of all that float,
  And his name's Admiral Death!

Which of you looks for a service free?
  (Hear what the sea-wind saith)
The rules o' the service are but three
  When ye sail with Admiral Death.
Steady your hand in time o' squalls,
Stand to the last by him that falls,
And answer clear to the voice that calls,
  " Ay, Ay! Admiral Death!"

How will ye know him among the rest?
  (Hear what the sea-wind saith)
By the glint o' the stars that cover his breast
  Ye may find Admiral Death.
By the forehead grim with an ancient scar,
By the voice that rolls like thunder far,
By the tenderest eyes of all that are,
  Ye may know Admiral Death.

Where are the lads that sailed before?   25
  (Hear what the sea-wind saith)
Their bones are white by many a shore,
  They sleep with Admiral Death.
Oh! but they loved him, young and old,
For he left the laggard, and took the bold,   30
And the fight was fought, and the story's told,
  And they sleep with Admiral Death.

SIR HENRY NEWBOLT

(*20th Century*)

1. Compare the last stanza of this poem with those of " He
   fell among Thieves " and " The Gay Gordons ".

2. Does this poem help you to understand Newbolt's attitude
   to death?

Notes : page 259.

POEMS

WITHOUT QUESTIONS OR COMMENTS

THE MOON IS UP

The moon is up : the stars are bright :
The wind is fresh and free !
We're out to seek for gold to-night
Across the silver sea !
The world was growing grey and old :   5
Break out the sails again !
We're out to seek a Realm of Gold
Beyond the Spanish Main.

We're sick of all the cringing knees,
The courtly smiles and lies !   10
God, let Thy singing Channel breeze
Lighten our hearts and eyes !
Let love no more be bought and sold
For earthly loss or gain :
We're out to seek an Age of Gold   15
Beyond the Spanish Main.

Beyond the light of far Cathay,
Beyond all mortal dreams,
Beyond the reach of night and day
Our El Dorado gleams,   20
Revealing—as the skies unfold—
A star without a stain,
The Glory of the Gates of Gold
Beyond the Spanish Main.

ALFRED NOYES
(*20th Century*)

ROADWAYS

One road leads to London,
  One road runs to Wales,
My road leads me seawards
  To the white dipping sails.

One road leads to the river,
  As it goes singing slow ;
My road leads to shipping,
  Where the bronzed sailors go.

Leads me, lures me, calls me
  To salt green tossing sea ;
A road without earth's road-dust
  Is the right road for me.

A wet road heaving, shining,
  And wild with seagulls' cries,
A mad salt sea-wind blowing
  The salt spray in my eyes.

My road calls me, lures me
  West, east, south, and north ;
Most roads lead men homewards,
  My road leads me forth :

To add more miles to the tally
  Of grey miles left behind,
In quest of that one beauty
  God put me here to find.

JOHN MASEFIELD
(*20th Century*)

FOR TO ADMIRE

The Injian Ocean sets an' smiles
  So sof', so bright, so bloomin' blue ;
There aren't a wave for miles an' miles
  Excep' the jiggle from the screw.
The ship is swep', the day is done,   5
  The bugle's gone for smoke and play ;
An' black ag'in the settin' sun
  The Lascar sings, " Hum deckty hai ! "

    For to admire an' for to see,
      For to be'old this world so wide—   10
    It never done no good to me,
      But I can't drop it if I tried !

I see the sergeants pitchin' quoits,
  I 'ear the women laugh an' talk,
I spy upon the quarter-deck   15
  The orficers an' lydies walk.
I thinks about the things that was,
  An' leans an' looks acrost the sea,
Till, spite of all the crowded ship,
  There's no one lef' alive but me.   20

The things that was which I 'ave seen,
  In barrick, camp, an' action too,
I tells them over by myself,
  An' sometimes wonders if they're true,
For they was odd—most awful odd—   25
  But all the same now they are o'er,
There must be 'eaps o' plenty such,
  An' if I wait I'll see some more.

" Hum deckty hai ! " : " *I'm looking out !* "

Oh, I 'ave come upon the books,
  An' frequent broke a barrick-rule,   30
An' stood beside an' watched myself
  Be'avin' like a bloomin' fool.
I paid my price for findin' out,
  Nor never grutched the price I paid,
But sat in Clink without my boots,   35
  Admirin' 'ow the world was made.

Be'old a cloud upon the beam,
  An' 'umped above the sea appears
Old Aden, like a barrick-stove
  That no one's lit for years an' years.   40
I passed by that when I began,
  An' I go 'ome the road I came,
A time-expired soldier-man
  With six years' service to 'is name.

My girl she said, " Oh, stay with me ! "   45
  My mother 'eld me to 'er breast.
They've never written none, an' so
  They must 'ave gone with all the rest—
With all the rest which I 'ave seen
  An' found an' known an' met along.   50
I cannot say the things I feel,
  And so I sing my evenin' song :

    For to admire an' for to see,
      For to be'old this world so wide—
    It never done no good to me,   55
      But I can't drop it if I tried !

RUDYARD KIPLING
(1865-1936)

THE FOX'S SKIN

When the wark's a' dune and the world's a' still,
And whaups are swoopin' across the hill,
And mither stands cryin', " Bairns, come ben,"
It's the time for the Hame o' the Pictish Men.

A sorrowfu' wind gaes up and doon, 5
An' me my lane in the licht o' the moon,
Gatherin' a bunch o' the flo'erin' whin,
Wi' my auld fur collar hapt roond my chin.

A star is shinin' on Morven Glen—
It shines on the Hame o' the Pictish Men. 10
Hither and yont their dust is blown,
But there's ane o' them keekin' ahint yon stone.

His queer auld face is wrinkled and riven,
Like a raggedy leaf, sae drookit and driven.
There's nocht to be feared at his ancient ways, 15
For this is a' that ever he says :

" The same auld wind at its weary cry :
The blin'-faced moon in the misty sky ;
A thoosand years o' clood and flame,
An' a'thing's the same an' aye the same— 20
The lass is the same in the fox's skin,
Gatherin' the bloom o' the flo'erin' whin".

MARION ANGUS
(*20th Century*)

whaups : *curlews*	hither and yont : *here and there*
come ben : *come in*	keekin' : *peeping*
my lane : *by myself*	ahint : *behind*
hapt : *wrapt*	drookit : *wet*

ON A ROMAN HELMET

(FOUND AT NEWSTEAD)

A helmet of the legion, this,
  That long and deep hath lain,
Come back to taste the living kiss
  Of sun and wind again.
Ah ! touch it with a reverent hand,   5
  For in its burnished dome
Lies here within this distant land
  The glory that was Rome !

The tides of sixteen hundred years
  Have flowed, and ebbed, and flowed,   10
And yet—I see the tossing spears
  Come up the Roman Road ;
While, high above the trumpets pealed,
  The eagles lift and fall,
And, all unseen, the war-god's shield   15
  Floats, guardian, over all !

Who marched beneath this gilded helm ?
  Who wore this casque a-shine ?
A leader mighty in the realm ?
  A soldier of the line ?   20
The proud patrician takes his rest
  The spearman's bones beside,
And earth who knows their secret best
  Gives this of all their pride !

With sunlight on this golden crest   25
  Maybe some Roman guard,
Set free from duty, wandered west
  Through Memory's gates unbarred ;
Or climbing Eildon cleft in three,
  Grown sick at heart for home,   30
Looked eastward to the grey North Sea
  That paved the way to Rome.

Or by the queen of Border streams
  That flowed his camp beneath
Long dallied with the dearer dreams   35
  Of love, as old as death,
And doffed his helm to dry lips' need,
  And dipped it in the tide,
And pledged in brimming wine of Tweed
  Some maid on Tiber-side.   40

Years pass : and Time keeps tally,
  And pride takes earth for tomb,
And down the Melrose valley
  Corn grows and roses bloom ;
The red suns set, the red suns rise,   45
  The ploughs lift through the loam,
And in one earth-worn helmet lies
  The majesty of Rome.

WILL. H. OGILVIE
(20*th Century*)

A SHIP, AN ISLE, A SICKLE MOON

A ship, an isle, a sickle moon—
With few but with how splendid stars
The mirrors of the sea are strewn
Between their silver bars !

  .   .   .

An isle beside an isle she lay,   5
The pale ship anchored in the bay,
While in the young moon's port of gold
A star-ship—as the mirrors told—
Put forth its great and lonely light
To the unreflecting Ocean, Night.   10
And still, a ship upon her seas,
The isle and the island cypresses
Went sailing on without the gale :
And still there moved the moon so pale,
A crescent ship without a sail !   15

JAMES ELROY FLECKER
(*20th Century*)

KUBLA KHAN

In Xanadu did Kubla Khan
A stately pleasure-dome decree :
Where Alph, the sacred river, ran
Through caverns measureless to man
  Down to a sunless sea.   5
So twice five miles of fertile ground
With walls and towers were girdled round :
And here were gardens bright with sinuous rills
Where blossomed many an incense-bearing tree :
And here were forests ancient as the hills,   10
Enfolding sunny spots of greenery.

But Oh ! that deep romantic chasm which slanted
Down the green hill athwart a cedarn cover !
A savage place ! as holy and enchanted
As e'er beneath a waning moon was haunted   15
By woman wailing for her demon-lover !
And from this chasm, with ceaseless turmoil seething,
As if this earth in fast thick pants were breathing,
A mighty fountain momently was forced :
Amid whose swift half-intermitted burst   20
Huge fragments vaulted like rebounding hail,
Or chaffy grain beneath the thresher's flail :
And 'mid these dancing rocks at once and ever
It flung up momently the sacred river.
Five miles meandering with a mazy motion   25
Through wood and dale the sacred river ran,
Then reached the caverns measureless to man,
And sank in tumult to a lifeless ocean :
And 'mid this tumult Kubla heard from far
Ancestral voices prophesying war !   30

The shadow of the dome of pleasure
Floated midway on the waves ;
Where was heard the mingled measure
From tne fountain and the caves.
It was a miracle of rare device,   35
A sunny pleasure-dome with caves of ice !

A damsel with a dulcimer
In a vision once I saw :
It was an Abyssinian maid,
And on her dulcimer she played,   40
Singing of Mount Abora.
Could I revive within me
Her symphony and song,
To such a deep delight 'twould win me,
That with music loud and long,   45
I would build that dome in air,
That sunny dome ! those caves of ice !
And all who heard should see them there,
And all should cry, Beware ! Beware !
His flashing eyes, his floating hair !   50
Weave a circle round him thrice,
And close your eyes with holy dread,
For he on honey-dew hath fed,
And drunk the milk of Paradise.

COLERIDGE
(1772-1834)

THE FISH-HAWK

On the large highway of the awful air that flows
  Unbounded between sea and heaven, while twilight
    screened
The sorrowful distances, he moved and had repose ;
  On the hugh wind of the Immensity he leaned
His steady body in long lapse of flight—and rose   5

Gradual, through broad gyres of ever-climbing rest,
  Up the clear stair of the eternal sky, and stood
Throned on the summit ! Slowly, with his widening
    breast,
  Widened around him the enormous Solitude,
From the grey rim of ocean to the glowing west.   10

Headlands and capes forlorn of the far coast, the land
  Rolling her barrens toward the south, he, from his
    throne
Upon the gigantic wind, beheld : he hung—he fanned
  The abyss for mighty joy, to feel beneath him strown
Pale pastures of the sea, with heaven on either hand— 15

The world with all her winds and waters, earth and air,
  Fields, folds, and moving clouds. The awful and
    adored
Arches and endless aisles of vacancy, the fair
  Void of sheer heights and hollows hailed him as her
    lord
And lover in the highest, to whom all heaven lay bare ! 20

Till from that tower of ecstasy, that baffled height,
  Stooping he sank ; and slowly on the world's wide
    way
Walked, with great wing on wing, the merciless, proud
    Might,
  Hunting the huddled and lone reaches for his prey
Down the dim shore—and faded in the crumbling light. 25

Slowly the dusk covered the land. Like a great hymn
  The sound of moving winds and waters was ; the sea
Whispered a benediction, and the west grew dim
  Where evening lifted her clear candles quietly . . .
Heaven, crowded with stars, trembled from rim to   30
  rim.

JOHN HALL WHEELOCK
(20th Century)

THE GREEN LINNET

Beneath these fruit-tree boughs that shed
Their snow-white blossoms on my head,
With brightest sunshine round me spread
  Of spring's unclouded weather,   5
In this sequestered nook how sweet
To sit upon my orchard-seat !
And birds and flowers once more to greet.
  My last year's friends together.

One have I marked, the happiest guest
In all this covert of the blest :   10
Hail to Thee, far above the rest
  In joy of voice and pinion !
Thou, Linnet ! in thy green array.
Presiding Spirit here to-day,
Dost lead the revels of the May ;   15
  And this is thy dominion.

While birds, and butterflies, and flowers,
Make all one band of paramours,
Thou, ranging up and down the bowers,
  Art sole in thy employment :   20
A Life, a Presence like the Air,
Scattering thy gladness without care,
Too blest with any one to pair ;
  Thyself thy own enjoyment.

124

Amid yon tuft of hazel-trees,   25
That twinkle to the gusty breeze,
Behold him perched in ecstasies,
    Yet seeming still to hover ;
There ! where the flutter of his wings
Upon his back and body flings
Shadows and sunny glimmerings,   30
    That cover him all over.

My dazzled sight he oft deceives,
A Brother of the dancing leaves ;
Then flits, and from the cottage-eaves   35
    Pours forth his song in gushes ;
As if by that exulting strain
He mocked and treated with disdain
The voiceless Form he chose to feign,
    While fluttering in the bushes.

WORDSWORTH
(1770-1850)

JENNY WREN

Of all the birds that rove and sing
    Near dwellings made for men.
None is so nimble, feat, and trim,
    As Jenny Wren.

With pin-point bill, and tail a-cock.   5
    So wildly shrill she cries,
The echoes on his roof-tree knock
    And fill the skies.

Never was sweeter seraph hid
    Within so small a house—   10
A tiny, inch-long, eager, ardent,
    Feathered mouse.

WALTER DE LA MARE
(20th Century)

THE KINGFISHER

It was the Rainbow gave thee birth,
   And left thee all her lovely hues ;
And, as her mother's name was Tears,
   So runs it in thy blood to choose
For haunts the lonely pools, and keep   5
In company with trees that weep.

Go you and, with such glorious hues,
   Live with proud Peacocks in green parks '
On lawns as smooth as shining glass,
   Let every feather show its marks ;   10
Get thee on boughs and clap thy wings
Before the windows of proud kings.

Nay, lovely bird, thou **art** not vain ;
   Thou hast no proud, ambitious mind :
I also love a quiet place   15
   That's green, away from all mankind ;
A lonely pool, and let a tree
Sigh with her bosom over me.

W. H. Davies
(20th Century)

TO THE GRASSHOPPER AND THE CRICKET

Green little vaulter in the sunny grass,
Catching your heart up at the feel of June,
Sole voice that's heard amidst the lazy noon,
When even the bees lag at the summoning brass;
And you, warm little housekeeper, who class   5
With those who think the candles come too soon,
Loving the fire, and with your tricksome tune
Nick the glad silent moments as they pass;

Oh sweet and tiny cousins, that belong,
One to the fields, the other to the hearth,   10
Both have your sunshine; both, though small,
    are strong
At your clear hearts; and both seem given to earth
To ring in thoughtful ears this natural song—
Indoors and out, summer and winter, mirth.

HUNT
(1784-1859)

ON THE GRASSHOPPER AND CRICKET

The poetry of earth is never dead:
When all the birds are faint with the hot sun,
And hide in cooling trees, a voice will run
From hedge to hedge about the new-mown mead;
That is the Grasshopper's—he takes the lead   5
In summer luxury—he has never done
With his delights; for, when tired out with fun,
He rests at ease beneath some pleasant weed.

The poetry of earth is ceasing never:
On a lone winter evening, when the frost   10
Has wrought a silence, from the stove there shrills
The Cricket's song, in warmth increasing ever,
And seems to one in drowsiness half-lost,
The Grasshopper's among some grassy hills.

KEATS
(1795-1821)

TO AUTUMN

Season of mists and mellow fruitfulness !
　　Close bosom-friend of the maturing sun ;
Conspiring with him how to load and bless
　　With fruit the vines that round the thatch-eaves
　　　　run ;
To bend with apples the moss'd cottage-trees,　　　　5
　　And fill all fruit with ripeness to the core ;
　　　　To swell the gourd, and plump the hazel shells
　　With a sweet kernel ; to set budding more,
And still more, later flowers for the bees,
Until they think warm days will never cease ;　　　　10
　　For Summer has o'erbrimm'd their clammy cells.

Who hath not seen thee oft amid thy store ?
　　Sometimes whoever seeks abroad may find
Thee sitting careless on a granary floor,
　　Thy hair soft-lifted by the winnowing wind ;　　　15
Or on a half-reap'd furrow sound asleep,
Drowsed with the fume of poppies, while thy hook
　　Spares the next swath and all its twinéd flowers ;
　　And sometimes like a gleaner thou dost keep
Steady thy laden head across a brook ;　　　　20
Or by a cider-press, with patient look,
　　Thou watchest the last oozings, hours by hours.

Where are the songs of Spring ?　Ay, where are they ?
　　Think not of them, thou hast thy music too,
While barréd clouds bloom the soft-dying day　　　25
　　And touch the stubble-plains with rosy hue ;
Then in a wailful choir the small gnats mourn
　　Among the river sallows, borne aloft
　　　　Or sinking as the light wind lives or dies ;
　　And full-grown lambs loud bleat from hilly bourn ;　30
Hedge-crickets sing ; and now with treble soft
The redbreast whistles from a garden-croft,
　　And gathering swallows twitter in the skies.

KEATS
(1795-1821)

From AUTUMNAL ODE

I saw old Autumn in the misty morn
Stand shadowless, like Silence, listening
To silence, for no lonely bird would sing
Into his hollow ear from woods forlorn,
Nor lowly hedge nor solitary thorn;   5
Shaking his languid locks all dewy bright
With tangled gossamer that fell by night,
   Pearling his coronet of golden corn.

Where are the songs of Summer?—With the sun,
Oping the dusky eyelids of the south,   10
Till Shade and Silence waken up as one,
And Morning sings with a warm odorous mouth.
Where are the merry birds?—Away, away,
On panting wings through the inclement skies,
      Lest owls should prey   15
      Undazzled at noonday,
And tear with horny beak their lustrous eyes.

Where are the blooms of Summer?—In the west,
Blushing their last to the last sunny hours,
When the mild Eve by sudden Night is prest   20
Like tearful Proserpine, snatch'd from her flowers
      To a most gloomy breast.
Where is the pride of Summer—the green prime—
The many, many leaves all twinkling?—Three
On the mossed elm; three on the naked lime,   25
Trembling; and one upon the old oak-tree!
   Where is the Dryads' immortality?
Gone into mournful cypress and dark yew,
Or wearing the long gloomy Winter through
   In the smooth holly's green eternity.   30

The squirrel gloats on his accomplished hoard,
The ants have brimmed their garners with ripe grain,
    And honey-bees have stored
The sweets of Summer in their luscious cells ;
The swallows all have wing'd across the main :   35
But here the Autumn melancholy dwells,
    And sighs her tearful spells
Amongst the sunless shadows of the plain.
        Alone, alone,
        Upon a mossy stone   40
She sits and reckons up the dead and gone
With the last leaves for a love-rosary,
Whilst all the wither'd world looks drearily,
Like a dim picture of the drownéd past
In the hushed mind's mysterious far away,   45
Doubtful what ghostly thing will steal the last
Into that distance, grey upon the grey.

HOOD
(1799-1845)

THE GOAT PATHS

(1)

The crooked paths
Go every way
Upon the hill
—They wind about
Through the heather
In and out
Of a quiet
Sunniness.

And the goats
Day after day,
Stray
In sunny
Quietness;
Cropping here,
And cropping there
—As they pause,
And turn,
And pass—
Now a bit
Of heather spray,
Now a mouthful
Of the grass.

(2)

In the deeper
Sunniness;
In the place
Where nothing stirs;
Quietly
In quietness;
In the quiet
Of the furze
They stand a while;
They dream;
They lie;
They stare
Upon the roving sky.

131

If you approach
They run away !
They will stare,
And stamp,
And bound,   40
With a sudden angry sound,
To the sunny
Quietude ;
To crouch again,
Where nothing stirs,   45
In the quiet
Of the furze :
To crouch them down again,
And brood,
In the sunny   50
Solitude.

(3)

Were I but
As free
As they,
I would stray   55
Away
And brood ;
I would beat
A hidden way,
Through the quiet,   60
Heather spray,
To a sunny solitude.

And should you come
I'd run away !
I would make an angry sound,   65
I would stare,
And stamp,
And bound
To the deeper
Quietude ;   70
To the place
Where nothing stirs

In the quiet
Of the furze.

(4)

In that airy   75
Quietness
I would dream
As long as they ;
Through the quiet
Sunniness   80
I would stray
Away
And brood,
All among
The heather spray,   85
In a sunny
Solitude.

—I would think
Until I found
Something   90
I can never find ;
—Something
Lying
On the ground,
In the bottom   95
Of my mind.

JAMES STEPHENS
(20th Century)

UP AT A VILLA—DOWN IN THE CITY

(*As Distinguished by an Italian Person of Quality*)

I

Had I but plenty of money, money enough and **to**
    spare,
The house for me, no doubt, were a house in the city
    square ;
Ah, such a life, such a life, as one leads at the window
    there !

II

Something to see, by Bacchus, something to hear, **at**
    least !
There, the whole day long, one's life is a perfect   5
    feast ;
While up at a villa one lives, I maintain it, no more
    than a beast.

III

Well now, look at our villa ! stuck like the horn of **a**
    bull
Just on a mountain's edge as bare as the creature's
    skull,
Save a mere shag of a bush with hardly a leaf to pull !
—I scratch my own, sometimes, to see if the hair's
    turned wool.   10

IV

But the city, oh the city—the square with the houses !
    Why ?
They are stone-faced, white as a curd, there's something
    to take the eye !
Houses in four straight lines, not a single front awry !
You watch who crosses and gossips, who saunters, who
    hurries by ;
Green blinds, as a matter of course, to draw when the
    sun gets high ;   15
And the shops with fanciful signs which are painted
    properly.

V

What of a villa ? Though winter be over in March by
    rights,
'Tis May perhaps ere the snow shall have withered well
    off the heights :
You've the brown ploughed land before, where the oxen
    steam and wheeze,
And the hills over-smoked behind by the faint grey
    olive-trees.   20

VI

Is it better in May, I ask you ? you've summer all at
    once ;
In a day he leaps complete with a few strong April
    suns !
'Mid the sharp short emerald wheat, scarce risen three
    fingers well,
The wild tulip, at end of its tube, blows out its great red
    bell
Like a thin clear bubble of blood, for the children to
    pick and sell.   25

VII

Is it ever hot in the square ? There's a fountain to spout
    and splash !
In the shade it sings and springs ; in the shine such
    foam-bows flash
On the horses with curling fish-tails, that prance
    and paddle and pash
Round the lady atop in the conch—fifty gazers do not
    abash,
Though all that she wears is some weeds round her
    waist in a sort of sash.   30

VIII

All the year long at the villa, nothing's to see though you
    linger,
Except yon cypress that points like Death's lean lifted
    forefinger.
Some think fireflies pretty, when they mix in the corn
    and mingle,
Or thrid the stinking hemp till the stalks of it seem
    a-tingle.
Late August or early September, the stunning cicala
    is shrill,   35
And the bees keep their tiresome whine round the
    resinous firs on the hill.
Enough of the seasons—I spare you the months of the
    fever and chill.

IX

Ere opening your eyes in the city, the blessed church-
    bells begin :
No sooner the bells leave off, than the diligence rattles
    in :
You get the pick of the news, and it costs you never a
    pin.   40
By and by there's the travelling doctor gives pills, lets
    blood, draws teeth ;
Or the Pulcinello-trumpet breaks up the market
    beneath.
At the post-office such a scene-picture—the new play,
    piping hot !
And a notice how, only this morning, three liberal
    thieves were shot.
Above it, behold the archbishop's most fatherly of
    rebukes,   45
And beneath, with his crown and his lion, some little
    new law of the Duke's !
Or a sonnet with flowery marge, to the Reverend Don
    So-and-so

136

Who is Dante, Boccaccio, Petrarcha, Saint Jerome, and
    Cicero,
" And moreover " (the sonnet goes rhyming) " the
    skirts of Saint Paul has reached,
Having preached us those six Lent Lectures more
    unctuous than ever he preached."   50
Noon strikes—here sweeps the procession ! our Lady
    borne smiling and smart
With a pink gauze gown all spangles, and seven swords
    stuck in her heart !
Bang, whang, whang goes the drum, *tootle-te-tootle*
    the fife ;
No keeping one's haunches still : it's the greatest
    pleasure in life.

X

But bless you, it's dear—it's dear ! fowls, wine, at
    double the rate.   55
They have clapped a new tax upon salt, and what oil
    pays passing the gate
It's a horror to think of. And so, the villa for me, not
    the city !
Beggars can scarcely be choosers : but still—ah, the
    pity, the pity !
Look, two and two go the priests, then the monks with
    cowls and sandals,
And the penitents dressed in white shirts, a-holding the
    yellow candles ;   60
One, he carries a flag up straight, and another a cross
    with handles,
And the Duke's guard brings up the rear, for the
    better prevention of scandals :
Bang, whang, whang goes the drum, *tootle-te-tootle*
    the fife.
Oh, a day in the city-square, there is no such pleasure
    in life !

BROWNING
(1812-1889)

137

From THE DESERTED VILLAGE

Near yonder copse, where once the garden smiled,
And still where many a garden-flower grows wild ;
There, where a few torn shrubs the place disclose,
The village preacher's modest mansion rose.
A man he was to all the country dear,   5
And passing rich with forty pounds a year ;
Remote from towns he ran his godly race,
Nor e'er had changed, nor wished to change, his place.
Unpractis'd he, to fawn ; or seek for power,
By doctrines fashion'd to the varying hour !   10
Far other aims his heart had learned to prize,
More skill'd to raise the wretched than to rise.

His house was known to all the vagrant train.
He chid their wand'rings, but relieved their pain.
The long remember'd beggar was his guest,   15
Whose beard descending swept his aged breast.
The ruin'd spendthrift, now no longer proud,
Claim'd kindred there, and had his claims allow'd.
The broken soldier, kindly bade to stay,
Sat by his fire, and talked the night away,   20
Wept o'er his wounds, or tales of sorrow done,
Shouldered his crutch and showed how fields were won.
Pleas'd with his guests, the good man learned to glow ;
And quite forgot their vices in their woe ;
Careless their merits or their faults to scan,   25
His pity gave ere charity began.

Thus to relieve the wretched was his pride,
And e'en his failings leaned to Virtue's side.
But, in his duty prompt at every call,
He watch'd and wept, he pray'd and felt, for all ;   30
And, as a bird each fond endearment tries
To tempt its new-fledg'd offspring to the skies,
He tried each art, reprov'd each dull delay,
Allur'd to brighter worlds, and led the way.

Beside the bed where parting life was laid,   35
And sorrow, guilt, and pain, by turns dismayed,
The reverend champion stood. At his control
Despair and anguish fled the struggling soul,
Comfort came down, the trembling wretch to raise,
And his last falt'ring accents whisper'd praise.   40

At church, with meek and unaffected grace,
His looks adorn'd the venerable place;
Truth from his lips prevail'd with double sway,
And fools, who came to scoff, remain'd to pray.
The service past, around the pious man,
With steady zeal, each honest rustic ran;   45
Even children follow'd with endearing wile,
And pluck'd his gown, to share the good man's smile.
His ready smile a parent's warmth express'd;
Their welfare pleas'd him, and their cares distress'd: 50
To them his heart, his love, his griefs were given,
But all his serious thoughts had rest in Heaven:
As some tall cliff, that lifts its awful form,
Swells from the vale, and midway leaves the storm,
Though round its breast the rolling clouds are spread,   55
Eternal sunshine settles on its head.

Beside yon straggling fence that skirts the way,
With blossom'd furze unprofitably gay,
There, in his noisy mansion, skill'd to rule,
The village master taught his little school;   60
A man severe he was, and stern to view;
I knew him well, and every truant knew:
Well had the boding tremblers learn'd to trace
The day's disasters in his morning face;
Full well they laugh'd with counterfeited glee   65
At all his jokes, for many a joke had he;
Full well the busy whisper, circling round,
Convey'd the dismal tidings when he frown'd.
Yet he was kind; or if severe in aught,
The love he bore to learning was in fault;   70
The village all declared how much he knew;

'Twas certain he could write, and cypher too ;
Lands he could measure, terms and tides presage,
And e'en the story ran that he could gauge :
In arguing, too, the parson own'd his skill,   75
For e'en though vanquish'd, he could argue still ;
While words of learned length and thund'ring sound
Amazed the gazing rustics rang'd around ;
And still they gaz'd, and still the wonder grew
That one small head could carry all he knew.   80
But past is all his fame.   The very spot
Where many a time he triumph'd, is forgot.

GOLDSMITH
(1728-1774)

WAR SONG OF THE SARACENS

We are they who come faster than fate : we are they who
    ride early or late :
We storm at your ivory gate : Pale Kings of the Sunset,
    beware !
Not on silk nor in samet we lie, not in curtained
    solemnity die
Among women who chatter and cry, and children who
    mumble a prayer.
But we sleep by the ropes of the camp, and we rise
    with a shout, and we tramp   5
With the sun or the moon for a lamp, and the spray
    of the wind in our hair.

From the lands, where the elephants are, to the
    forts of Merou and Balghar,
Our steel we have brought and our star to shine on
    the ruins of Rum.
We have marched from the Indus to Spain, and by
    God we will go there again ;
We have stood on the shore of the plain where the
    Waters of Destiny boom.   10
A mart of destruction we made at Jalula where men were
    afraid,
For death was a difficult trade, and the sword was a
    broker of doom ;

And the Spear was a Desert Physician who cured not
    a few of ambition,
And drave not a few to perdition with medicine bitter
    and strong :
And the shield was a grief to the fool and as bright as
    a desolate pool,   15
And as straight as the rock of Stamboul when their
    cavalry thundered along :
For the coward was drowned with the brave when our
    battle sheered up like a wave,
And the dead to the desert we gave, and the glory to
    God in our song.

James Elroy Flecker
(*20th Century*)

From THE BATTLE OF NASEBY

Oh ! wherefore come ye forth, in triumph from the
   North,
  With your hands, and your feet, and your raiment all
   red ?
And wherefore doth your rout send forth a joyous
   shout ?
  And whence be the grapes of the wine-press which
   ye tread ?

Oh evil was the root, and bitter was the fruit,   5
  And crimson was the juice of the vintage that we
   trod ;
For we trampled on the throng of the haughty and
   the strong,
  Who sate in the high places, and slew the saints of
   God.

It was about the noon of a glorious day of June,
  That we saw their banners dance, and their cuirasses
   shine,   10
And the Man of Blood was there, with his long essencéd
   hair,
  And Astley, and Sir Marmaduke, and Rupert of
   the Rhine.

Like a servant of the Lord, with his Bible and his
   sword,
  The General rode along us to form us to the fight,
When a murmuring sound broke out, and swell'd
   into a shout,   15
  Among the godless horsemen upon the tyrant's right.

And hark ! like the roar of the billows on the shore,
  The cry of battle rises along their charging line !
For God ! for the Cause ! for the Church ! for the
   Laws !
  For Charles King of England, and Rupert of the
   Rhine !   20

The furious German comes, with his clarions and his
    drums,
  His bravoes of Alsatia, and pages of Whitehall ;
They are bursting on our flanks. Grasp your pikes,
    close your ranks ;
  For Rupert never comes but to conquer or to fall.

They are here ! They rush on ! We are broken !
    We are gone !   25
  Our left is borne before them like stubble on the
    blast.
O Lord put forth Thy might. O Lord defend the
    right !
  Stand back to back, in God's name, and fight it to
    the last.

Stout Skippon hath a wound ; the centre hath given
    ground :
  Hark ! hark !—What means the trampling of horse-
    men on our rear ?   30
Whose banner do I see, boys ? 'Tis he, thank God, 'tis
    he, boys.
  Bear up another minute ; brave Oliver is here.

Their heads all stooping low, their points all in a
    row,
  Like a whirlwind on the trees, like a deluge on the
    dykes,
Our cuirassiers have burst on the ranks of the Accurst, 35
  And at a shock have scattered the forest of his pikes.

MACAULAY
(1800-1859)

From MARCHING ALONG

Kentish Sir Byng stood for his King,
Bidding the crop-headed Parliament swing:
And, pressing a troop unable to stoop
And see the rogues flourish and honest folk droop,
Marched them along, fifty-score strong,
Great-hearted gentlemen, singing this song.

God for King Charles! Pym and such carles
To the Devil that prompts 'em their treasonous parles!
Cavaliers, up! Lips from the cup,
Hands from the pasty, nor bite take nor sup
Till you're—

  Chorus— *Marching along, fifty-score strong,*
      Great-hearted gentlemen, singing this song.

Then, God for King Charles! Pym and his snarls
To the Devil that pricks on such pestilent carles!
Hold by the right, you double your might;
So, onward to Nottingham, fresh for the fight,

  Chorus— *March we along, fifty-score strong,*
      Great-hearted gentlemen, singing this song!

BROWNING
(1812-1889)

144

TO-MORROW

Oh yesterday the cutting edge drank thirstily and deep,
The upland outlaws ringed us in and herded us as
    sheep,
They drove us from the stricken field and bayed us
    into keep;
        But to-morrow,
  By the living God, we'll try the game again!   5

Oh yesterday our little troop was ridden through and
    through,
Our swaying, tattered pennons fled, a broken, beaten
    few
And all a summer afternoon they hunted us and slew;
        But to-morrow,
  By the living God, we'll try the game again!   10

And here upon the turret-top the bale-fire glowers
    red,
The wake-lights burn and drip about our hacked,
    disfigured dead,
And many a broken heart is here and many a broken
    head;
        But to-morrow,
  By the living God, we'll try the game again!   15

JOHN MASEFIELD
(*20th Century*)

KINMONT WILLIE

O have ye na heard o' the fause Sakelde?
  O have ye na heard o' the keen Lord Scroope?
How they hae ta'en bauld Kinmont Willie,
  On Haribee to hang him up?

Had Willie had but twenty men,   5
  But twenty men as stout as he,
Fause Sakelde had never the Kinmont ta'en,
  Wi' eight score in his companie.

They band his legs beneath the steed,
  They tied his hands behind his back;   10
They guarded him, fivesome on each side,
  And they brought him owre the Liddel-rack.

They led him through the Liddle-rack,
  And also through the Carlisle sands;
They brought him to Carlisle castle,   15
  To be at my Lord Scroope's commands.

" My hands are tied, but my tongue is free,
  And wha will dare this deed avow?
Or answer by the Border law?
  Or answer to the bauld Buccleuch? "   20

" Now haud thy tongue, thou rank reiver !
  There's never a Scot shall set ye free;
Before ye cross my castle-yett,
  I trow ye shall take farewell o' me."

reiver : *robber*   trow : *trust*
castle-yett : *castle-gate*

" Fear na ye that, my lord," quo' Willie ;   25
    " By the faith o' my body, Lord Scroope," he said,
" I never yet lodged in a hostelrie
    But I paid my lawing before I gaed."

Now word is gane to the bauld Keeper,
    In Branksome Ha' where that he lay,   30
That Lord Scroope has ta'en the Kinmont Willie,
    Between the hours of night and day.

He has ta'en the table wi' his hand,
    He gar'd the red wine spring on hie ;
" Now Christ's curse on my head," he said,   35
    " But avengéd of Lord Scroope I'll be !

" O is my basnet a widow's curch ?
    Or my lance a wand of the willow-tree ?
Or my arm a lady's lily hand,
    That an English lord should lightly me ?   40

" And have they ta'en him, Kinmont Willie,
    Against the truce of Border tide,
And forgotten that the bauld Buccleuch
    Is Keeper here on the Scottish side ?

" And have they e'en ta'en him, Kinmont Willie,   45
    Withouten either dread or fear,
And forgotten that the bauld Buccleuch
    Can back a steed, or shake a spear ?

" O were there war between the lands,
    As well I wot that there is none,   50
I would slight Carlisle castle high,
    Though it were builded of marble-stone.

lawing : *reckoning*   curch : *head-dress*
basnet : *helmet*

" I would set that castle in a lowe,
   And sloken it with English blood ;
There's never a man in Cumberland   55
   Should ken where Carlisle castle stood.

" But since nae war's between the lands,
   And there is peace, and peace should be,
I'll neither harm English lad or lass,
   And yet the Kinmont freed shall be ! "   60

He has called him forty marchmen bauld,
   I trow they were of his ain name,
Except Sir Gilbert Elliot, called
   The Laird of Stobs, I mean the same.

He has called him forty marchmen bauld,   65
   Were kinsmen to the bauld Buccleuch ;
With spur on heel, and splent on spauld,
   And gloves of green, and feathers blue.

There were five and five before them a',
   Wi' hunting-horns and bugles bright ;   70
And five and five came wi' Buccleuch,
   Like Warden's men, arrayed for fight.

And five and five like a mason gang
   That carried the ladders lang and hie ;
And five and five like broken men ;   75
   And so they reached the Woodhouselee.

And as we crossed the 'Bateable Land,
   When to the English side we held,
The first o' men that we met wi',
   Wha should it be but fause Sakelde ?   80

lowe : *blaze*   splent on spauld : *armour on shoulder*
sloken : *quench*   broken men : *homeless men*
'Bateable land : *Debateable Land—No Man's Land*

" Where be ye gaun, ye hunters keen ? "
    Quo' fause Sakelde ; " come tell to me ! "
" We go to hunt an English stag
    Has trespassed on the Scots countrie."

" Where be ye gaun, ye marshal men ? "   85
    Quo' fause Sakelde ; " come tell me true ! "
" We go to catch a rank reiver,
    Has broken faith wi' the bauld Buccleuch."

" Where be ye gaun, ye mason lads,
    Wi' a' your ladders, lang and hie ? "   90
" We gang to herry a corbie's nest,
    That wons not far from Woodhouselee."

" Where be ye gaun, ye broken men ? "
    Quo' fause Sakelde ; " come tell to me ! "
Now Dickie of Dryhope led that band,   95
    And the never a word of lear had he.

" Why trespass ye on the English side ?
    Row-footed outlaws, stand ! " quo' he ;
The never a word had Dickie to say,
    Sae he thrust the lance thro' his fause bodie.   100

Then on we held for Carlisle toun,
    And at Staneshaw-bank the Eden we crossed ;
The water was great and muckle of spate,
    But the never a horse nor man we lost.

And when we reached the Staneshaw-bank,   105
    The wind was rising loud and hie ;
And there the laird gar'd leave our steeds,
    For fear that they should stamp and neigh.

herry : *harry*   corbie : *raven*   wons : *dwells*

And when we left the Staneshaw-bank,
    The wind began fu' loud to blaw ;   110
But 'twas wind and weet, and fire and sleet,
    When we came beneath the castle wa'.

We crept on knees, and held our breath,
    Till we placed the ladders against the wa' ;
And sae ready was Buccleuch himsel'   115
    To mount the first before us a' ;

He has ta'en the watchman by the throat,
    He flung him down upon the lead :
" Had there not been peace between our lands,
    Upon the other side thou'dst gaed.   120

" Now sound out, trumpets ! " quo' Buccleuch ;
" Let's waken Lord Scroope right merrilie ! "
Then loud the Warden's trumpets blew—
    O wha daur meddle wi' me?

Then speedilie to wark we gaed,   125
    And raised the slogan ane and a',
And cut a hole thro' a sheet of lead,
    And so we wan to the castle ha'.

They thought King James and a' his men
    Had won the house wi' bow and spear :   130
It was but twenty Scots and ten
    That put a thousand in sic a steir.

Wi' coulters and wi' forehammers,
    We gar'd the bars bang merrilie,
Until we came to the inner prison,   135
    Where Willie o' Kinmont he did lie.

steir : *stir*

And when we came to the lower prison,
  Where Willie o' Kinmont he did lie,
" O sleep ye, wake ye, Kinmont Willie,
  Upon the morn that thou's to die ? "   140

" O I sleep saft, and I wake aft ;
  It's lang since sleeping was fleyed frae me !
Gie my service back to my wife and bairns,
  And a' gude fellows that speir for me."

Then Red Rowan has hent him up,   145
  The starkest man in Teviotdale :
" Abide, abide now, Red Rowan,
  Till of my Lord Scroope I take farewell."

" Farewell, farewell, my gude Lord Scroope !
  My gude Lord Scroope, farewell ! " he cried ; 150
" I'll pay you for my lodging mail,
  When first we meet on the Border side."

Then shoulder high, with shout and cry.
  We bore him down the ladder lang ;
At every stride Red Rowan made   155
  I wot the Kinmont's airns played clang.

" O mony a time," quo' Kinmont Willie,
  " I have ridden horse baith wild and wud ;
But a rougher beast than Red Rowan
  I ween my legs have ne'er bestrode."   160

" And mony a time," quo' Kinmont Willie,
  " I've pricked a horse out owre the furs ;
But since the day I backed a steed,
  I never wore sic cumbrous spurs "

fleyed : *frightened*	mail : *rent*
speir : *enquire*	wud : *mad*
hent : *taken*	furs : *furrows*

We scarce had won the Staneshaw-Bank, 165
 When a' the Carlisle bells were rung,
And a thousand men on horse and foot
 Came wi' the keen Lord Scroope along.

Buccleuch has turned to Eden Water,
 Even where it flowed frae bank to brim, 170
And he has plunged in wi' a' his band,
 And safely swam them through the stream.

He turned him on the other side,
 And at Lord Scroope his glove flung he :
" If ye like na my visit in merrie England, 175
 In fair Scotland come visit me ! "

All sore astonished stood Lord Scroope,
 He stood as still as rock of stane ;
He scarcely dared to trow his eyes,
 When through the water they had gane. 180

" He is either himsel' a devil frae hell,
 Or else his mother a witch maun be ;
I wadna have ridden that wan water
 For a' the gowd in Christentie."

ANONYMOUS

THE BATTLE OF OTTERBURN

It fell about the Lammas tide,
  When the muir-men win their hay,
The doughty Douglas bound him to ride
  Into England, to drive a prey.

He chose the Gordons and the Græmes,   5
  With them the Lindsays, light and gay ;
But the Jardines wald not with him ride,
  And they rue it to this day.

And he has burned the dales of Tyne,
  And part of Bambrough-shire ;   10
And three good towers on Reidswire fells,
  He left them all on fire.

And he marched up to Newcastle,
  And rode it round about ;
" O wha's the lord of this castle,   15
  Or wha's the lady o't ? "

But up spake proud Lord Percy, then,
  And O but he spake hie !
" I am the lord of this castle,
  My wife's the lady gay."   20

" If thou'rt the lord of this castle,
  Sae weel it pleases me !
For, ere I cross the border fells,
  The tane of us shall die."

He took a long spear in his hand,   25
  Shod with the metal free,
And for to meet the Douglas there
  He rode right furiouslie.

Lammas tide : *1st August*   win : *harvest*
muir-men : *moor-men*

But O how pale his lady look'd
   Frae aff the castle wa',   30
When down, before the Scottish spear,
   She saw proud Percy fa'.

" Had we twa been upon the green,
   And never an eye to see,
I wad hae had you, flesh and fell ;   35
   But your sword sall gae wi' me."

" But gae ye up to Otterburn,
   And wait there dayis three ;
And, if I come not ere three dayis end,
   A fause knight ca' ye me."   40

" The Otterburn's a bonnie burn ;
   'Tis pleasant there to be ;
But there is nought at Otterburn
   To feed my men and me.

" The deer rins wild on hill and dale,   45
   The birds fly wild from tree to tree ;
But there is neither bread nor kail
   To fend my men and me.

" Yet I will stay at Otterburn,
   Where you shall welcome be :   50
And, if ye come not at three dayis end,
   A fause lord I'll ca' thee."

" Thither will I come," proud Percy said,
   " By the might of Our Lady ! "—
" There will I bide thee," said the Douglas,   55
   " My trowth I plight to thee."

hie : *haughtily*	kail : *broth*
the tane : *the one*	fend : *supply*

They lighted high on Otterburn,
  Upon the bent sae brown ;
They lighted high on Otterburn,
  And threw their pallions down.   60

And he that had a bonnie boy,
  Sent out his horse to grass ;
And he that had not a bonnie boy,
  His ain servant he was.

But up then spake a little page,   65
  Before the peep of dawn—
" O waken ye, waken ye, my good lord,
For Percy's hard at hand."

" Ye lie, ye lie, ye liar loud !
  Sae loud I hear ye lie :   70
For Percy had not men yestreen,
  To dight my men and me.

" But I hae dream'd a dreary dream,
  Beyond the Isle of Sky :
I saw a dead man win a fight,   75
  And I think that man was I."

He belted on his good braid sword,
  And to the field he ran ;
But he forgot the helmet good,
  That should have kept his brain.   80

When Percy wi' the Douglas met,
  I wot he was fu' fain !
They swakked their swords, till sair they swat,
  And the blood ran down like rain.

pallions : *tents*   dight : *drub*
swakked : *clashed*

But Percy with his good broad sword,
  That could so sharply wound,
Has wounded Douglas on the brow,
  Till he fell to the ground.

Then he call'd on his little foot-page,
  And said—" Run speedilie,
And fetch my ain dear sister's son,
  Sir Hugh Montgomery."

" My nephew good," the Douglas said,
  " What recks the death of ane !
Last night I dream'd a dreary dream,
  And I ken the day's thy ain.

" My wound is deep ; I fain would sleep ;
  Take thou the vanguard of the three,
And hide me by the braken bush,
  That grows on yonder lily lea.

" O bury me by the braken bush,
  Beneath the blooming brier,
Let never living mortal ken
  That ere a kindly Scot lies here."

He lifted up that noble lord,
  Wi' the saut tear in his e'e ;
He hid him in the braken bush,
  That his merrie men might not see.

The moon was clear, the day drew near,
  The spears in flinders flew,
But many a gallant Englishman
  Ere day the Scotsmen slew.

flinders : *splinters*

The Gordons good, in English blood
  They steeped their hose and shoon ;
The Lindsays flew like fire about,   115
  Till all the fray was done.

The Percy and Montgomery met,
  That either of other were fain ;
They swakked swords, and they twa swat,
  And aye the blude ran down between.   120

" Yield thee, O yield thee, Percy ! " he said,
  " Or else I vow I'll lay thee low ! "
" Whom to shall I yield," said Earl Percy,
  " Now that I see it must be so ? "

" Thou shalt not yield to lord nor loun,   125
  Nor yet shalt thou yield to me ;
But yield thee to the braken bush,
  That grows upon yon lily lea ! "

" I will not yield to a braken bush,
  Nor yet will I yield to a brier ;   130
But I would yield to Earl Douglas,
  Or Sir Hugh Montgomery, if he were here."

As soon as he knew it was Montgomery,
  He struck his sword's point in the ground ;
And the Montgomery was a courteous knight,   135
  And quickly took him by the honde.

This deed was done at Otterburn,
  About the breaking of the day ;
Earl Douglas was buried at the braken bush,
  And the Percy led captive away.   140

ANONYMOUS

loun : *commoner*

157

YE BANKS AND BRAES O' BONNIE DOON

Ye banks and braes o' bonnie Doon,
　How can ye bloom sae fresh and fair !
How can ye chant, ye little birds,
　And I sae weary, fu' o' care !
Thou'll break my heart, thou warbling bird　　　5
　That wantons thro' the flowering thorn :
Thou minds me o' departed joys,
　Departed, never to return.

Aft hae I rov'd by bonnie Doon,
　To see the rose and woodbine twine ;　　　10
And ilka bird sang o' its luve,
　And fondly sae did I o' mine ;
Wi' lightsome heart I pu'd a rose,
　Fu' sweet upon its thorny tree ;
And my fause luver staw my rose,　　　15
　But, ah ! he left the thorn wi' me,

Burns
(1759-1796)

ilka : *every*　　　staw : *stole*　　　fause : *false*

YE FLOWERY BANKS O' BONNIE DOON

Ye flowery banks o' bonnie Doon
　How can ye bloom sae fair !
How can ye chant, ye little birds,
　And I sae fu' o' care !

Thou'll break my heart, thou bonnie bird　　　5
　That sings upon the bough ;
Thou minds me o' the happy days
　When my fause luve was true.

158

Thou'll break my heart, thou bonnie bird
   That sings beside thy mate;   10
For sae I sat, and sae I sang,
   And wistna o' my fate.

Aft hae I roved by bonnie Doon
   To see the woodbine twine,
And ilka bird sang o' its luve;   15
   And sae did I o' mine.

Wi' lightsome heart I pu'd a rose,
   Frae aff its thorny tree;
And my fause luver staw the rose,
   But left the thorn wi' me.   20

BURNS
(1759-1796)

minds : *remindest*.   wistna : *knew not*

JOHN ANDERSON

John Anderson, my jo, John,
   When we were first acquent,
Your locks were like the raven,
   Your bonnie brow was brent :
But now your brow is bald, John,   5
   Your locks are like the snow,
But blessings on your frosty pow.
   John Anderson, my jo !

John Anderson, my jo, John,
   We clamb the hill thegither,   10
And mony a canty day, John,
   We've had wi' ane anither ;
Now we maun totter down, John,
   And hand in hand we'll go,
And sleep thegither at the foot,   15
   John Anderson, my jo !

BURNS
(1759-1796)

jo : *love*   pow : *head*
brent : *unwrinkled*   canty : *happy*

BRIGNALL BANKS

O Brignall banks are wild and fair,
  And Greta woods are green,
And you may gather garlands there
  Would grace a summer queen.
And as I rode by Dalton-Hall,   5
  Beneath the turrets high,
A Maiden on the castle wall
  Was singing merrily :

" O Brignall banks are fresh and fair,
  And Greta woods are green ;   10
I'd rather rove with Edmund there
  Than reign our English queen."

" If, Maiden, thou wouldst wend with me
  To leave both tower and town,
Thou first must guess what life lead we   15
  That dwell by dale and down.
And if thou canst that riddle read,
  As read full well you may,
Then to the greenwood shalt thou speed
  As blithe as Queen of May."   20

Yet sung she, " Brignall banks are fair,
  And Greta woods are green ;
I'd rather rove with Edmund there
  Than reign our English queen.

" I read you, by your bugle-horn   25
  And by your palfrey good,
I read you for a ranger sworn
  To keep the king's greenwood."
" A ranger, lady, winds his horn,
  And 'tis at peep of light ;   30
His blast is heard at merry morn,
  And mine at dead of night."

Yet sung she, " Brignall banks are fair,
  And Greta woods are gay ;
I would I were with Edmund there
  To reign his Queen of May !   35

" With burnished brand and musketoon,
  So gallantly you come,
I read you for a bold Dragoon
  That lists the tuck of drum."   40
" I list no more the tuck of drum,
  No more the trumpet hear ;
But when the beetle sounds his hum
  My comrades take the spear.

" And O ! though Brignall banks be fair   45
  And Greta woods be gay,
Yet mickle must the maiden dare
  Would reign my Queen of May !

" Maiden ! a nameless life I lead,
  A nameless death I'll die !   50
The fiend whose lantern lights the mead
  Were better mate than I !
And when I'm wth my comrades met
  Beneath the greenwood bough,
What once we were we all forget,   55
  Nor think what we are now.

" Yet Brignall banks are fresh and fair,
  And Greta woods are green,
And you may gather garlands there
  Would grace a summer queen."   60

SCOTT
(1771-1832)

THE ROVER

" A weary lot is thine, fair maid,
  A weary lot is thine !
To pull the thorn thy brow to braid,
  And press the rue for wine !
A lightsome eye, a soldier's mien,   5
  A feather of the blue,
A doublet of the Lincoln green—
  No more of me you knew,
    My Love !
No more of me you knew.   10

"The morn is merry June, I trow,
  The rose is budding fain ;
But she shall bloom in winter snow
  Ere we two meet again."
He turned his charger as he spake,   15
  Upon the river shore,
He gave the bridle-reins a shake,
  Said, " Adieu for evermore,
    My Love !
And adieu for evermore."   20

SCOTT
(1771-1832)

TO S. R. CROCKETT

Blows the wind to-day, and the sun and the rain are
    flying,
  Blows the wind on the moors to-day and now,
Where about the graves of the martyrs the whaups
    are crying,
  My heart remembers how !

Grey recumbent tombs of the dead in desert places,   5
  Standing stones on the vacant wine-red moor,
Hills of sheep, and the howes of the silent vanished
    races,
  And winds, austere and pure :

Be it granted me to behold you again in dying,
  Hills of home ! and to hear again the call ;   10
Hear about the graves of the martyrs the peewees
    crying,
  And hear no more at all.

R. L. Stevenson
(1850-1894)

whaups : *curlews*   peewees : *lapwings*
howes : *either valleys or barrows*

IN THE HIGHLANDS, IN THE COUNTRY PLACES

In the highlands, in the country places,
Where the old plain men have rosy faces,
  And the young fair maidens
    Quiet eyes ;
Where essential silence cheers and blesses,   5
And for ever in the hill-recesses
  Her more lovely music
    Broods and dies.

O to mount again where erst I haunted ;
Where the old red hills are bird-enchanted,   10
  And the low green meadows
    Bright with sward ;
And when even dies, the million-tinted,
And the night has come, and planets glinted.
  Lo, the valley hollow   15
    Lamp-bestarred !

O to dream, O to awake and wander
There, and with delight to take and render,
  Through the trance of silence,
    Quiet breath ;   20
Lo ! for there, among the flowers and grasses,
Only the mightier movement sounds and passes ;
  Only winds and rivers,
    Life and death.

R. L. Stevenson
(1850-1894)

CANADIAN BOAT SONG

Listen to me, as when ye heard our father
    Sing long ago the song of other shores ;
Listen to me, and then in chorus gather
    All your deep voices as ye pull your oars :

Fair these broad meads—these hoary woods are grand ;   5
But we are exiles from our father's land.

From the lone shieling of the misty island
    Mountains divide us, and the waste of seas ;
Yet still the blood is strong, the heart is Highland,
    And we in dreams behold the Hebrides.   10

We ne'er shall tread the fancy-haunted valley,
    Where 'tween the dark hills creeps the small clear
        stream ;
In arms around the patriarch banner rally,
    Nor see the moon on royal tombstones gleam.

When the bold kindred, in the time long-vanish'd,   15
    Conquer'd the soil and fortified the keep,
No seer foretold the children would be banish'd,
    That a degenerate lord might boast his sheep.

Come foreign rage—let Discord burst in slaughter !
    O then for clansmen true, and stern claymore !   20
The hearts that would have given their blood like water
    Beat heavily beyond the Atlantic roar.

Fair these broad meads—these hoary woods are grand ;
But we are exiles from our father's land.

ANONYMOUS

THE HOWE O' THE MEARNS

Laddie, my lad, when ye gang at the tail o' the plough
      An' the days draw in,
When the burnin' yellow's awa' that was aince a-lowe
      On the braes o' whin,
Do ye mind o' me that's deaved wi' the wearyfu' south   5
      An' it's puir consairns,
While the weepies fade on the knowes at the river's
   mouth
      In the Howe o' the Mearns?

There was nae twa lads frae the Grampians doon to the
   Tay
      That could best us twa;   10
At bothie or dance, or the field on a fitba' day,
      We could sort them a';
An' at courtin'-time when the stars keeked doon on the
   glen
      An' its theek o' fairns,
It was you an' me got the pick o' the basket then   15
      In the Howe o' the Mearns.

London is fine, an' for ilk o' the lassies at hame
      There'll be saxty here,
But the springtime comes an' the hairst—an' it's aye
   the same
      Through the changefu' year.   20
O, a lad thinks lang o' hame ere he thinks his fill
      As his breid he airns—
An' they're thrashin' noo at the white fairm up on the
   hill
      In the Howe o' the Mearns.

tail o' the plough : *behind the plough*   keeked : *peeped*

alowe : *aflame*   theek : *thatch*

deaved : *deafened*   hairst : *harvest*

weepies : *ragwort*

Gin I mind mysel' an' toil for the lave o' my days   25
      While I've een to see,
When I'm auld an' done wi' the fash o' their English
  ways
      I'll be hame to dee ;
For the lad dreams aye o' the prize that the man 'll get,
      But he lives an' lairns,   30
An' it's far, far ayont him still—but it's farther yet
      To the Howe o' the Mearns.

Laddie, my lad, when the hair is white on your pow
      An' the work's put past,
When your hand's owre auld an' heavy to haud the
  plough   35
      I'll win hame at last,
And we'll bide our time on the knowes whaur the broom
  stands braw
      An' we played as bairns,
Till the last lang gloamin' shall creep on us baith an'
  fa'
      On the Howe o' the Mearns.   40

VIOLET JACOB
(20th Century)

gin : *if*   lave : *remainder*   fash : *worry*

From THE COTTAR'S SATURDAY NIGHT

From scenes like these old Scotia's grandeur springs
  That makes her loved at home, revered abroad :
Princes and lords are but the breath of kings,
  " An honest man's the noblest work of God ! "
And certes, in fair virtue's heavenly road,   5
  The cottage leaves the palace far behind :
What is a lordling's pomp ?—a cumbrous load,
  Disguising oft the wretch of human kind,
Studied in arts of hell, in wickedness refined !

Oh Scotia ! my dear, my native soil !   10
  For whom my warmest wish to Heaven is sent,
Long may thy hardy sons of rustic toil
  Be blest with health, and peace, and sweet content !
And, Oh ! may Heaven their simple lives prevent
  From luxury's contagion, weak and vile !   15
Then, howe'er crowns and coronets be rent,
  A virtuous populace may rise the while,
And stand a wall of fire around their much-loved Isle.

BURNS
(1759-1796)

THE BULL-FIGHT

Hush'd is the din of tongues—on gallant steeds,
With milk-white crest, gold spur, and light-poised
   lance,
Four cavaliers prepare for venturous deeds,
And lowly bending to the lists advance ;
Rich are their scarfs, their chargers featly prance :   5
If in the dangerous game they shine to-day,
The crowd's loud shout and ladies' lovely glance,
Best prize of better acts, they bear away,
And all that kings or chiefs e'er gain their toils repay.

In costly sheen and gaudy cloak array'd,   10
But all afoot, the light-limb'd Matadore
Stands in the centre, eager to invade
The lord of lowing herds ; but not before
The ground, with cautious tread, is traversed o'er,
Lest aught unseen should lurk to thwart his speed :   15
His arms a dart, he fights aloof, nor more
Can man achieve without the friendly steed—
Alas ! too oft condemn'd for him to bear and bleed.

Thrice sounds the clarion ; lo ! the signal falls,
The den expands, and Expectation mute   20
Gapes round the silent circle's peopled walls.
Bounds with one lashing spring the mighty brute,
And wildly staring, spurns, with sounding foot,
The sand, nor blindly rushes on his foe :
Here, there, he points his threatening front, to suit   25
His first attack, wide waving to and fro
His angry tail ; red rolls his eye's dilated glow.

Sudden he stops; his eye is fix'd: away,
Away, thou heedless boy! prepare the spear;
Now is thy time, to perish, or display   30
The skill that yet may check his mad career.
With well-timed croupe the nimble coursers veer;
On foams the bull, but not unscathed he goes;
Streams from his flank the crimson torrent clear:
He flies, he wheels, distracted with his throes: 35
Dart follows dart; lance, lance; loud bellowings speak
    his woes . . .

Foil'd, bleeding, breathless, furious to the last,
Full in the centre stands the bull at bay,
Mid wounds, and clinging darts, and lances brast,
And foes disabled in the brutal fray: 40
And now the Matadores around him play,
Shake the red cloak, and poise the ready brand:
Once more through all he bursts his thundering
    way—
Vain rage! the mantle quits the conynge hand,
Wraps his fierce eye—'tis past—he sinks upon the
    sand!   45

Where his vast neck just mingles with the spine,
Sheathed in his form the deadly weapon lies.
He stops—he starts—disdaining to decline:
Slowly he falls, amidst triumphant cries,
Without a groan, without a struggle dies.   50
The decorated car appears—on high
The corse is piled—sweet sight for vulgar eyes—
Four steeds that spurn the rein, as swift as shy,
Hurl the dark bulk along, scarce seen in dashing by.

("Childe Harold's Pilgrimage", *Canto I, Stanzas LXXIII-LXXVI,
    LXXVIII-LXXIX.*)

BYRON
(1788-1824)

Stop ! for thy tread is on an Empire's dust !
An earthquake's spoil is sepulchred below !
Is the spot mark'd with no colossal bust ?
Nor column trophied for triumphal show ?
None ; but the moral's truth tells simpler so.   5
As the ground was before, thus let it be ;
How that red rain hath made the harvest grow !
And is this all the world has gain'd by thee,
Thou first and last of fields ! king-making Victory ! . . .

There was a sound of revelry by night,   10
And Belgium's capital had gather'd then
Her Beauty and her Chivalry, and bright
The lamps shone o'er fair women and brave men ;
A thousand hearts beat happily ; and when
Music arose with its voluptuous swell,   15
Soft eyes look'd love to eyes which spake again,
And all went merry as a marriage-bell ;
But hush ! hark ! a deep sound strikes like a rising
    knell !

Did ye not hear it ?—No ; 'twas but the wind,
Or the car rattling o'er the stony street ;   20
On with the dance ! let joy be unconfined ;
No sleep till morn, when Youth and Pleasure meet
To chase the glowing Hours with flying feet.
But hark !—that heavy sound breaks in once more,
As if the clouds its echo would repeat ;   25
And nearer, clearer, deadlier than before !
Arm ! arm ! it is—it is—the cannon's opening roar !

Within a window'd niche of that high hall
Sate Brunswick's fated chieftain ; he did hear
That sound, the first amidst the festival   30
And caught its tone with Death's prophetic ear ;
And when they smiled because he deem'd it near,
His heart more truly knew that peal too well
Which stretch'd his father on a bloody bier,
And roused the vengeance blood alone could quell ;   35
He rush'd into the field, and, foremost fighting, fell.

Ah ! then and there was hurrying to and fro,
And gathering tears, and tremblings of distress,
And cheeks all pale, which but an hour ago
Blush'd at the praise of their own loveliness ;   40
And there were sudden partings, such as press
The life from out young hearts, and choking sighs
Which ne'er might be repeated ; who could guess
If ever more should meet those mutual eyes,
Since upon night so sweet such awful morn could   45
    rise !

And there was mounting in hot haste : the steed,
The mustering squadron, and the clattering car,
Went pouring forward with impetuous speed,
And swiftly forming in the ranks of war ;
And the deep thunder peal on peal afar ;   50
And near, the beat of the alarming drum
Roused up the soldier ere the morning star ;
While throng'd the citizens with terror dumb,
Or whispering, with white lips—" The foe ! they
    come ! they come ! "

And wild and high the " Cameron's Gathering "
   rose !   55
The war-note of Lochiel, which Albyn's hills
Have heard, and heard, too, have her Saxon foes :
How in the noon of night that pibroch thrills,
Savage and shrill ! But with the breath which fills
Their mountain-pipe, so fill the mountaineers   60
With the fierce native daring which instils
The stirring memory of a thousand years,
And Evan's, Donald's fame rings in each clansman's
   ears !

And Ardennes waves above them her green leaves,
Dewy with nature's tear-drops, as they pass,   65
Grieving, if aught inanimate e'er grieves,
Over the unreturning brave—alas !
Ere evening to be trodden like the grass
Which now beneath them, but above shall grow
In its next verdure, when this fiery mass   70
Of living valour, rolling on the foe,
And burning with high hope, shall moulder cold and
   low.

Last noon beheld them full of lusty life,
Last eve in Beauty's circle proudly gay,
The midnight brought the signal-sound of strife,   75
The morn the marshalling in arms—the day
Battle's magnificently stern array !
The thunder-clouds close o'er it, which when rent
The earth is cover'd thick with other clay,
Which her own clay shall cover, heap'd and pent,   80
Rider and horse—friend, foe—in one red burial blent !

(" Childe Harold's Pilgrimage ", *Canto III, Starzas XVII, XXI-
XXVIII.*)

BYRON
(1788-1824)

THE BALLAD OF EAST AND WEST

*Oh, East is East, and West is West, and never the twain
shall meet,*
*Till Earth and Sky stand presently at God's great
Judgment Seat;*
*But there is neither East nor West, Border, nor Breed,
nor Birth,*
*When two strong men stand face to face, tho' they come from
the ends of the earth!*

Kamal is out with twenty men to raise the Border-side, 5
And he has lifted the Colonel's mare that is the Colonel's
pride:
He has lifted her out of the stable-door between the
dawn and the day,
And turned the calkins upon her feet, and ridden her
far away.
Then up and spoke the Colonel's son that led a troop
of the Guides:
" Is there never a man of all my men can say where
Kamal hides? " 10
Then up and spoke Mahommed Khan, the son of the
Ressaldar:
" If ye know the track of the morning-mist, ye know
where his pickets are.
At dusk he harries the Abazai—at dawn he is into
Bonair,
But he must go by Fort Bukloh to his own place to
fare,
So if ye gallop to Fort Bukloh as fast as a bird can
fly, 15
By the favour of God ye may cut him off ere he win
to the Tongue of Jagai.
But if he be past the Tongue of Jagai, right swiftly
turn ye then,
For the length and the breadth of that grisly plain is
sown with Kamal's men.

There is rock to the left, and rock to the right, and
    low lean thorn between,
And ye may hear a breech-bolt snick where never a
    man is seen."   20
The Colonel's son has taken a horse, and a raw rough
    dun was he,
With the mouth of a bell and the heart of Hell and
    the head of the gallows-tree.
The Colonel's son to the Fort has won, they bid him
    stay to eat—
Who rides at the tail of a Border thief, he sits not
    long at his meat.
He's up and away from Fort Bukloh as fast as he can
    fly,   25
Till he was aware of his father's mare in the gut of the
    Tongue of Jagai,
Till he was aware of his father's mare with Kamal
    upon her back,
And when he could spy the white of her eye, he made
    the pistol crack.
He has fired once, he has fired twice, but the whistling
    ball went wide.
" Ye shoot like a soldier," Kamal said. " Show now
    if ye can ride."   30
It's up and over the Tongue of Jagai, as blown dust-
    devils go,
The dun he fled like a stag of ten, but the mare like
    a barren doe.
The dun he leaned against the bit and slugged his
    head above,
But the red mare played with the snaffle-bars, as a
    maiden plays with a glove. .
There was rock to the left and rock to the right, and
    low lean thorn between,   35
And thrice he heard a breech-bolt snick tho' never a
    man was seen.
They have ridden the low moon out of the sky, their
    hoofs drum up the dawn ;
The dun he went like a wounded bull, but the mare
    like a new-roused fawn.

The dun he fell at a watercourse—in a woful heap
    fell he,
And Kamal has turned the red mare back, and pulled
    the rider free.   40
He has knocked the pistol out of his hand—small
    room was there to strive ;
" 'Twas only by favour of mine," quoth he, " ye rode
    so long alive :
There was not a rock for twenty mile, there was not a
    clump of tree,
But covered a man of my own men with his rifle cocked
    on his knee.
If I had raised my bridle-hand, as I have held it low, 45
The little jackals that flee so fast were feasting all in a
    row ;
If I had bowed my head on my breast, as I have held
    it high,
The kite that whistles above us now were gorged till
    she could not fly."
Lightly answered the Colonel's son : " Do good to
    bird and beast,
But count who come for the broken meats before thou
    makest a feast.   50
If there should follow a thousand swords to carry my
    bones away,
Belike the price of a jackal's meal were more than a
    thief could pay.
They will feed their horse on the standing crop, their
    men on the garnered grain,
The thatch of the byres will serve their fires when all
    the cattle are slain.
But if thou thinkest the price be fair—thy brethren
    wait to sup,   55
The hound is kin to the jackal-spawn—howl, dog, and
    call them up !
And if thou thinkest the price be high, in steer and
    gear and stack,
Give me my father's mare again, and I'll fight my
    own way back ! "

Kamal has gripped him by the hand and set him upon
        his feet.
" No talk shall be of dogs," said he, " when wolf and
        grey wolf meet.   60
May I eat dirt if thou hast hurt of me in deed or
        breath ;
What dam of lances brought thee forth to jest at the
        dawn with Death ? "
Lightly answered the Colonel's son : " I hold by the
        blood of my clan :
Take up the mare for my father's gift—by God, she
        has carried a man ! "
The red mare ran to the Colonel's son, and nuzzled
        against his breast :   65
" We be two strong men," said Kamal then, "but she
        loveth the younger best.
So she shall go with a lifter's dower, my turquoise-
        studded rein,
My broidered saddle and saddle-cloth, and silver
        stirrups twain."
The Colonel's son a pistol drew and held it muzzle-
        end,
" Ye have taken the one from a foe," said he ; " will
        ye take the mate from a friend ? "   70
" A gift for a gift," said Kamal straight ; " a limb for
        the risk of a limb.
Thy father has sent his son to me, I'll send my son to
        him ! "
With that he whistled his only son, that dropped from
        a mountain-crest—
He trod the ling like a buck in spring, and he looked
        like a lance in rest.
" Now here is thy master," Kamal said, " who leads a
        troop of the Guides,   75
And thou must ride at his left side as shield on
        shoulder rides.
Till Death or I cut loose the tie, at camp and board
        and bed,
Thy life is his—thy fate it is to guard him with thy
        head.

So, thou must eat the White Queen's meat, and all
        her foes are thine,
And thou must harry thy father's hold for the peace
        of the Border-line,   80
And thou must make a trooper tough and hack thy way
        to power—
Belike they will raise thee to Ressaldar when I am
        hanged in Peshawur."

They have looked each other between the eyes, and
        there they found no fault,
They have taken the Oath of the Brother-in-Blood on
        leavened bread and salt :
They have taken the Oath of the Brother-in-Blood on
        fire and fresh-cut sod,   85
On the hilt and the haft of the Khyber knife, and the
        Wondrous Names of God.
The Colonel's son he rides the mare and Kamal's boy
        the dun,
And two have come back to Fort Bukloh where there
        went forth but one.
And when they drew to the Quarter-Guard, full
        twenty swords flew clear—
There was not a man but carried his feud with the
        blood of the mountaineer.   90
" Ha' done ! ha' done ! " said the Colonel's son.
        " Put up the steel at your sides !
Last night ye had struck at a Border thief—to-night
        'tis a man of the Guides ! "

*Oh, East is East, and West is West, and never the twain
        shall meet,*
*Till Earth and Sky stand presently at God's great
        Judgment Seat ;*
*But there is neither East nor West, Border, nor Breed,
        nor Birth,*   95
*When two strong men stand face to face, tho' they come
        from the ends of the earth !*

Rudyard Kipling
(1865-1936)

178

PACK, CLOUDS, AWAY!

Pack, clouds, away! and welcome, day!
　　With night we banish sorrow:
Sweet air, blow soft! mount, lark, aloft!
　　To give my Love good-morrow!
Wings from the wind, to please her mind,　　5
　　Notes from the lark I'll borrow.
Bird, prune thy wing! nightingale, sing!
　　To give my Love good-morrow.
　　To give my Love good-morrow,
　　Notes from them all I'll borrow.　　10

Wake from thy nest, robin red-breast!
　　Sing, birds, in every furrow!
And from each bill let music shrill
　　Give my fair Love good-morrow.
Blackbird and thrush, in every bush,　　15
　　Stare, linnet, and cock-sparrow,
You pretty elves, among yourselves
　　Sing my fair Love good-morrow!
　　To give my Love good-morrow,
　　Sing, birds, in every furrow!

HEYWOOD
(157?-1650)

stare : *starling*

TO DIANEME

Sweet, be not proud of those two eyes
Which starlike sparkle in their skies;
Nor be you proud that you can see
All hearts your captives; yours yet free:
Be you not proud of that rich hair
Which wantons with the love-sick air;　　5
Whenas that ruby which you wear,
Sunk from the tip of your soft ear,
Will last to be a precious stone
When all your world of beauty's gone.　　10

HERRICK
(1591-1674)

THERE IS A LADY SWEET AND KIND

There is a Lady sweet and kind,
Was never face so pleased my mind;
I did but see her passing by,
And yet I love her till I die.

Her gesture, motion, and her smiles,
Her wit, her voice my heart beguiles,
Beguiles my heart, I know not why,
And yet I love her till I die.

Cupid is wingéd and doth range,
Her country so my love doth change :
But change she earth, or change she sky,
Yet will I love her till I die.

From THOMAS FORD's *Music of Sundry Kinds*, 1607

LOVE NOT ME FOR COMELY GRACE

Love not me for comely grace,
For my pleasing eye or face,
Nor for any outward part,
No, nor for a constant heart :
   For these may fail or turn to ill,
     So thou and I shall sever :
Keep, therefore, a true woman's eye,
And love me still but know not why—
   So hast thou the same reason still
     To doat upon me ever !

From JOHN WILBYE's *Second Set of Madrigals*, 1609

SERENA SINGS

In March I loved a farmer's boy
  When lusty winds were blowing;
Upon the downs we took our joy
  Where violets were growing.
I said, " When springtime's left the hill,
When rose has routed daffodil,
Sweet shepherd, will you love me still? "
  He answered, " There's no knowing."
     No knowing,
     No knowing;
He answered, " There's no knowing."

In June I loved a soldier lad—
  We kissed without delaying :
I swear as bold a way he had
  Of wooing as of slaying.
I said, " When skies have lost their blue,
When summer bids us all adieu,
Sweet soldier, will you love me true? "
  He answered, " There's no saying."
     No saying,
     No saying;
He answered, " There's no saying."

When autumn came I loved a man
  Who had nor trade nor dwelling :
In Nonepass Wood our love began,
  And, oh ! 'twas all excelling.
I said, " When autumn's red and gold
Are trodden into winter's mould,
Sweet gipsy, will your love grow cold? "
  He answered, " There's no telling."
     No telling,
     No telling;
He answered, " There's no telling".

Now she who'd 'scape a broken heart
  Must love to suit the season :   35
And when two lovers come to part
  Let neither talk of treason.
Who knows that winter may not bring
As good as left you in the spring ?
For love's a light and chancy thing
  That's got no rhyme or reason.   40
      No reason,
      No reason ;
That's got no rhyme or reason.

JAN STRUTHER
(*20th Century*)
(*From "Punch"*)

HEY NONNY NO !

Hey nonny no !
Men are fools that wish to die !
Is't not fine to dance and sing
When the bells of death do ring ?
Is't not fine to swim in wine,   5
And turn upon the toe,
And sing hey nonny no !
When the winds blow and the seas flow ?
Hey nonny no !

ANONYMOUS

THE LOVER'S RESOLUTION

Shall I, wasting in despair,
Die because a woman's fair?
Or make pale my cheek with care
'Cause another's rosy are?
Be she fairer than the day,   5
Or the flow'ry meads in May,
    If she think not well of me,
    What care I how fair she be?

Shall my silly heart be pined
'Cause I see a woman kind?   10
Or a well disposéd nature
Joinéd with a lovely feature?
Be she meeker, kinder, than
Turtle-dove or pelican,
    If she be not so to me,   15
    What care I how kind she be?

Shall a woman's virtues move
Me to perish for her love?
Or her well-deservings known
Make me quite forget my own?
Be she with that goodness blest   20
Which may merit name of Best,
    If she be not such to me,
    What care I how good she be?

'Cause her fortune seems too high,	25
Shall I play the fool and die?
She that bears a noble mind,
If not outward helps she find,
Thinks what with them he would do
That without them dares her woo;	30
    And unless that mind I see,
    What care I how great she be?

Great, or good, or kind, or fair,
I will ne'er the more despair;
If she love me, this believe,	35
I will die ere she shall grieve;
If she slight me when I woo,
I can scorn and let her go;
    For if she be not for me,
    What care I for whom she be?	40

WITHER
(1588-1667)

ELIZABETH OF BOHEMIA

You meaner beauties of the night,
   That poorly satisfy our eyes
More by your number than your light,
   You common people of the skies ;
   What are you when the moon shall rise ?   5

You curious chanters of the wood,
   That warble forth Dame Nature's lays,
Thinking your passions understood
   By your weak accents ; what's your praise
   When Philomel her voice shall raise ?   10

You violets that first appear,
   By your pure purple mantles known
Like the proud virgins of the year,
   As if the spring were all your own ;
   What are you when the rose is blown ?   15

So, when my mistress shall be seen
   In form and beauty of her mind,
By virtue first, then choice, a Queen,
   Tell me, if she were not design'd
   Th' eclipse and glory of her kind.   20

WOTTON
(1568-1639)

HYMN TO DIANA

Queen and huntress, chaste and fair,
   Now the sun is laid to sleep,
Seated in thy silver chair,
   State in wonted manner keep :
Hesperus entreats thy light,   5
Goddess excellently bright.

185

Earth, let not thy envious shade
  Dare itself to interpose ;
Cynthia's shining orb was made
  Heaven to clear when day did close :   10
Bless us then with wishéd sight,
Goddess excellently bright.

Lay thy bow of pearl apart,
  And thy crystal-shining quiver ;
Give unto the flying hart   15
  Space to breathe, how short soever :
Thou that mak'st a day of night,
Goddess excellently bright.

JONSON
(1573-1637)

TO CELIA

Drink to me only with thine eyes,
  And I will pledge with mine ;
Or leave a kiss but in the cup,
  And I'll not look for wine.
The thirst that from the soul doth rise   5
  Doth ask a drink divine ;
But might I of Jove's nectar sup,
  I would not change for thine.

I sent thee late a rosy wreath,
  Not so much honouring thee   10
As giving it a hope that there
  It could not wither'd be ;
But thou thereon didst only breathe
  And sent'st it back to me ;
Since when it grows, and smells, I swear,   15
  Not of itself but thee !

JONSON
(1573-1637)

186

TAKE, O TAKE THOSE LIPS AWAY

Take, O take those lips away
　　That so sweetly were forsworn,
And those eyes, the break of day,
　　Lights that do mislead the morn !
But my kisses bring again,　　　　　　　　　　　5
　　　　　　Bring again ;
Seals of love, but seal'd in vain,
　　　　　　Seal'd in vain !

SHAKESPEARE
(1564-1616)

COME AWAY, COME AWAY, DEATH

Come away, come away, death,
　　And in sad cypres let me be laid ;
Fly away, fly away, breath ;
　　I am slain by a fair cruel maid.
My shroud of white, stuck all with yew,　　　　　5
　　　　　　O prepare it !
My part of death, no one so true
　　　　　　Did share it.

Not a flower, not a flower sweet,
　　On my black coffin let there be strown ;　　　10
Not a friend, not a friend greet
　　My poor corse, where my bones shall be thrown :
A thousand thousand sighs to save,
　　　　　　Lay me, O, where
Sad true lover never find my grave　　　　　　15
　　　　　　To weep there !

SHAKESPEARE
(1564-1616)

cypres : *crape*

ST. CRISPIN'S DAY

WESTMORELAND. O that we now had here
But one ten thousand of those men in England
That do no work to-day !

KING HENRY.   What's he that wishes so ?
My cousin Westmoreland ? No, my fair cousin :
If we are marked to die, we are enow   5
To do our country loss ; and if to live,
The fewer men, the greater share of honour.
God's will ! I pray thee, wish not one man more.
By Jove, I am not covetous for gold,
Nor care I who doth feed upon my cost ;   10
It yearns me not if men my garments wear ;
Such outward things dwell not in my desires :
But if it be a sin to covet honour,
I am the most offending soul alive.
No, faith, my coz, wish not a man from England :   15
God's peace ! I would not lose so great an honour
As one man more, methinks, would share from me,
For the best hope I have. O, do not wish one more !
Rather proclaim it, Westmoreland, through my host,
That he which hath no stomach to this fight,   20
Let him depart ; his passport shall be made,
And crowns for convoy put into his purse :
We would not die in that man's company
That fears his fellowship to die with us.
This day is called the feast of Crispian :   25
He that outlives this day, and comes safe home,
Will stand a-tip-toe when this day is named,
And rouse him at the name of Crispian.
He that shall live this day, and see old age,
Will yearly on the vigil feast his neighbours,   30
And say, " To-morrow is Saint Crispian : "
Then will he strip his sleeve and show his scars,
And say, " These wounds I had on Crispin's day."
Old men forget ; yet all shall be forgot,
But he'll remember with advantages   35
What feats he did that day : then shall our names,

Familiar in his mouth as household words,
Harry the King, Bedford and Exeter,
Warwick and Talbot, Salisbury and Gloucester,
Be in their flowing cups freshly remembered.   40
This story shall the good man teach his son ;
And Crispin Crispian shall ne'er go by,
From this day to the ending of the world,
But we in it shall be rememberéd ;
We few, we happy few, we band of brothers ;   45
For he to-day that sheds his blood with me
Shall be my brother ; be he ne'er so vile,
This day shall gentle his condition :
And gentlemen in England now a-bed
Shall think themselves accursed they were not here,   50
And hold their manhoods cheap whiles any speaks
That fought with us upon Saint Crispin's day.

("HENRY V")   SHAKESPEARE
                                           (1564-1616)

GAUNT'S SPEECH

This royal throne of kings, this scepter'd isle,
This earth of majesty, this seat of Mars,
This other Eden, demi-paradise,
This fortress built by Nature for herself
Against infection and the hand of war,   5
This happy breed of men, this little world,
This precious stone set in the silver sea,
Which serves it in the office of a wall
Or as a moat defensive to a house,
Against the envy of less happier lands,   10
This blessed plot, this earth, this realm, this England,
This nurse, this teeming womb of royal kings,
Fear'd by their breed and famous by their birth,
Renownéd for their deeds as far from home,

For Christian service and true chivalry,   15
As is the sepulchre in stubborn Jewry
Of the world's ransom, blessed Mary's Son,
This land of such dear souls, this dear dear land,
Dear for her reputation through the world,
Is now leased out, I die pronouncing it,   20
Like to a tenement or pelting farm :
England, bound in with the triumphant sea,
Whose rocky shore beats back the envious siege
Of watery Neptune, is now bound in with shame,
With inky blots and rotten parchment bonds :   25
That England, that was wont to conquer others,
Hath made a shameful conquest of itself.
Ah, would the scandal vanish with my life,
How happy then were my ensuing death !

("RICHARD II")   SHAKESPEARE
                                                        (1564-1616)

pelting : *mean, paltry*

From KING JOHN

This England never did, nor never shall,
Lie at the proud foot of a conqueror,
But when it first did help to wound itself.
Now these her princes are come home again,
Come the three corners of the world in arms,   5
And we shall shock them. Nought shall make us rue,
If England to itself do rest but true.
                                                        SHAKESPEARE
                                                        (1564-1616)

Come listen to me, you gallants so free,
   All you that love mirth for to hear,
And I will tell you of a bold outlaw
   That lived in Nottinghamshire.

As Robin Hood in the forest stood,   5
   All under the greenwood tree,
There was he ware of a brave young man
   As fine as fine might be.

The youngster was clothed in scarlet red,
   In scarlet fine and gay ;   10
And he did frisk it over the plain,
   And chanted a roundelay.

As Robin Hood next morning stood
   Amongst the leaves so gay,
There did he spy the same young man,   15
   Come drooping along the way.

The scarlet he wore the day before,
   It was clean cast away ;
At every step he fetched a sigh—
   " Alack and a well-a-day ! "   20

Then stepped forth brave Little John,
   And Much, the miller's son,
Which made the young man bend his bow,
   When as he saw them come.

"Stand off, stand off!" the young man said,   25
    "What is your will with me?"
"You must come before our master straight,
    Under yon greenwood tree."

And when he came bold Robin before,
    Robin asked him courteously,   30
"Oh, hast thou any money to spare
    For my merry men and me?"

"I have no money," the young man said,
    "But five shillings and a ring;
And that I have kept this seven long years,   35
    To have it at my wedding.

"Yesterday I should have married a maid,
    But she soon from me was ta'en,
And chosen to be an old knight's bride,
    Whereby my poor heart is slain."   40

"What is thy name?" then said Robin Hood,
    "Come tell me without any fail."
"By the faith of my body," then said the young man,
    "My name it is Allan-a-Dale."

"What wilt thou give me?" said Robin Hood,   45
    "In ready gold or fee,
To help thee to thy true love again,
    And deliver her unto thee?"

"I have no money," then quoth the young man,
    "No ready gold nor fee,   50
But I will swear upon a book
    Thy true servant for to be."

"How many miles is it to thy true love?
    Come tell me without guile."
"By the faith of my body," then said the young man, 55
    "It is but five little mile."

Then Robin he hasted over the plain,
    He did neither stint nor lin,
Until he came unto the church,
    Where Allan should keep his wedding.   60

"What dost thou here?" the bishop then said,
    "I prithee now tell to me."
"I am a bold harper," quoth Robin Hood,
    "And the best in the north countree."

"O welcome, O welcome!" the bishop said;   65
    "That music best pleaseth me."
"You shall have no music," quoth Robin Hood,
    "Till the bride and the bridegroom I see."

With that came in a wealthy knight,
    Which was both grave and old,   70
And after him a handsome lass,
    That shone like the glistering gold.

"This is not a fit match," quoth bold Robin Hood,
    "That you do seem to make here,
For since we are come into the church,   75
    The bride shall choose her own dear."

Then Robin Hood put his horn to his mouth,
    And blew blasts two or three;
When four-and-twenty bowmen bold
    Came leaping over the lea.   80

stint : *pause*   lin : *stop*

And when they came into the churchyard,
   Marching all in a row,
The first man was Allan-a-Dale,
   To give bold Robin his bow.

" This is thy true love," then Robin said,   85
   " Young Allan, as I hear say ;
And you shall be married at this same time
   Before we depart away."

" That shall not be," the bishop said,
   " For thy word shall not stand ;   90
They shall be three times asked in the church,
   As the law is of our land."

Robin Hood pulled off the bishop's coat,
   And put it on Little John ;
" By the faith of my body," then Robin said,   95
   " This cloth doth make thee a man."

When Little John went into the quire,
   The people began to laugh ;
He asked them seven times in the church,
   Lest three should not be enough.   100

" Who gives this maid ? " said Little John ;
   Quoth Robin, " That do I.
And he that takes her from Allan-a-Dale,
   Full dearly he shall her buy."

And thus having ended this merry wedding,   105
   The bride looked like a queen ;
And so they returned to the merry greenwood,
   Amongst the leaves so green.

ANONYMOUS

194

SHERWOOD

Sherwood in the twilight, is Robin Hood awake?
Grey and ghostly shadows are gliding through the
    brake,
Shadows of the dappled deer, dreaming of the morn,
Dreaming of a shadowy man that winds a shadowy
    horn.

Robin Hood is here again : all his merry thieves 5
Hear a ghostly bugle-note shivering through the leaves,
Calling as he used to call, faint and far away,
In Sherwood, in Sherwood, about the break of day.

Merry, merry England has kissed the lips of June :
All the wings of fairyland are here beneath the moon. 10
Like a flight of rose-leaves fluttering in a mist
Of opal and ruby and pearl and amethyst.

Merry, merry England is waking as of old,
With eyes of blither hazel and hair of brighter gold :
For Robin Hood is here again beneath the bursting
    spray, 15
In Sherwood, in Sherwood, about the break of day.

Love is in the greenwood building him a house
Of wild rose and hawthorn and honeysuckle boughs :
Love is in the greenwood, dawn is in the skies,
And Marian is waiting with a glory in her eyes. 20

Hark ! The dazzled laverock climbs the golden steep !
Marian is waiting : is Robin Hood asleep ?
Round the fairy grass-rings frolic elf and fay,
In Sherwood, in Sherwood, about the break of day.

Oberon, Oberon, rake away the gold, 25
Rake away the red leaves, roll away the mould,
Rake away the gold leaves, roll away the red,
And wake Will Scarlett from his leafy forest bed.

Friar Tuck and Little John are riding down together
With quarter-staff and drinking-can and grey goose
      feather.   30
The dead are coming back again, the years are rolled
      away
In Sherwood, in Sherwood, about the break of day.

Softly over Sherwood the south wind blows.
All the heart of England hid in every rose
Hears across the greenwood the sunny whisper leap,   35
Sherwood in the red dawn, is Robin Hood asleep ?

Hark ! the voice of England wakes him as of old,
And, shattering the silence with a cry of brighter gold,
Bugles in the greenwood echo from the steep,
Sherwood in the red dawn, is Robin Hood asleep?   40

Where the deer are gliding down the shadowy glen,
All across the glades of fern he calls his merry men—
Doublets of the Lincoln-green glancing through the
      May
In Sherwood, in Sherwood, about the break of day—

Calls them and they answer : from aisles of oak and
      ash   45
Rings the *Follow ! Follow !* and the boughs begin to
      crash,
The ferns begin to flutter and the flowers begin to fly,
And through the crimson dawning the robber band
      goes by.

Robin ! Robin ! Robin ! All his merry thieves
Answer as the bugle-note shivers through the leaves,   50
Calling as he used to call, faint and far away,
In Sherwood, in Sherwood, about the break of day.

ALFRED NOYES
(*20th Century*)

WHEN THE TRAVELLER RETURNS

When the traveller returns
And the voyage is o'er,
How the heart in him burns,
How sweet is the shore
With the hills of his youth, and the fields, and the
flowers that his footsteps restore.   5

But the spell of the past
And the spell of the main
That were over him cast,
Will they speak not again,
In the sound of the trees and the waters, in the noise
of the wind and the rain?   10

In the ears of the child
From his taking of breath
Is the voice of the wild
And the word that it saith,
Though the prize be a longing unslaked, and the price
of it danger and death.   15

W. MACNEILE DIXON
(*20th Century*)

A WAR SONG TO ENGLISHMEN

Prepare, prepare the iron helm of war,
Bring forth the lots, cast in the spacious orb;
The Angel of Fate turns them with mighty hands,
And casts them out upon the darkened earth.
     Prepare, prepare.   5

Prepare your hearts for Death's cold hand! prepare
Your souls for flight, your bodies for the earth!
Prepare your arms for glorious victory.
Prepare your eyes to meet a holy God.
     Prepare, prepare.   10

Whose fatal scroll is that? Methinks 'tis mine.
Why sinks my heart, why faltereth my tongue?
Had I three lives, I'd die in such a cause.
And rise, with ghosts, over the well-fought field.
     Prepare, prepare.   15

The arrows of Almighty God are drawn,
Angels of Death stand in the low'ring heavens.
Thousands of souls must seek the realms of light,
And walk together on the clouds of heaven.
     Prepare, prepare.   20

Soldiers, prepare! Our cause is Heaven's cause;
Soldiers, prepare! Be worthy of our cause:
Prepare to meet our fathers in the sky:
Prepare, O troops that are to fall to-day.
     Prepare, prepare.   25

Alfred shall smile, and make his heart rejoice;
The Norman William and the learned Clerk,
And Lion-Heart, and black-browed Edward with
His loyal queen, shall rise, and welcome us.   30
     Prepare, prepare.

BLAKE
(1757-1827)

ENGLAND, MY ENGLAND

What have I done for you,
    England, my England?
What is there I would not do,
    England, my own?
With your glorious eyes austere,
As the Lord were walking near,
Whispering terrible things and dear
    As the Song on your bugles blown,
    England—
    Round the world on your bugles blown!

Where shall the watchful Sun,
    England, my England,
Match the master-work you've done,
    England, my own?
When shall he rejoice again
Such a breed of mighty men
As come forward, one to ten,
    To the Song on your bugles blown,
    England—
    Down the years on your bugles blown?

Ever the faith endures,
    England, my England:
" Take and break us : we are yours,
    England, my own!
Life is good, and joy runs high
Between English earth and sky :
Death is death ; but we shall die
    To the Song on your bugles blown,
    England—
    To the stars on your bugles blown ! "

They call you proud and hard,
    England, my England :
You with worlds to watch and ward,
    England, my own!

You whose mailed hand keeps the keys   35
Of such teeming destinies,
You could know nor dread nor ease
    Were the Song on your bugles blown,
    England,
    Round the Pit on your bugles blown !   40

Mother of Ships whose might,
    England, my England,
Is the fierce old Sea's delight,
    England, my own,
Chosen daughter of the Lord,   45
Spouse-in-Chief of the ancient sword,
There's the menace of the Word
    In the Song on your bugles blown,
    England—
    Out of heaven on your bugles blown !   50

HENLEY
(1849-1903)

JERUSALEM

And did those feet in ancient time
   Walk upon England's mountain green?
And was the holy Lamb of God
   On England's pleasant pastures seen?

And did the Countenance Divine   5
   Shine forth upon our clouded hills?
And was Jerusalem builded here
   Among these dark Satanic mills?

Bring me my bow of burning gold!
   Bring me my arrows of desire!   10
Bring me my spear: O clouds, unfold!
   Bring me my chariot of fire!

I will not cease from mental fight,
   Nor shall my sword sleep in my hand,
Till we have built Jerusalem   15
   In England's green and pleasant land.

BLAKE
(1757-1827)

EVERYONE SANG

Everyone suddenly burst out singing;
And I was filled with such delight
As prisoned birds must find in freedom
Winging wildly across the white
Orchards and dark green fields; on; on; and out
   of sight.   5

Everyone's voice was suddenly lifted,
And beauty came like the setting sun.
My heart was shaken with tears, and horror
Drifted away. . . . O, but every one
Was a bird; and the song was wordless; the singing
   will never be done.   10

SIEGFRIED SASSOON
(20th Century)

A windy night was blowing on Rome,
The cressets guttered on Caesar's home,
The fish-boats, moored at the bridge, were breaking
The rush of the river to yellow foam.

The hinges whined to the shutters shaking,   5
When clip-clop-clep came a horse-hoof raking
The stones of the road at Caesar's gate ;
The spear-butts jarred at the guard's awaking.

" Who goes there ? " said the guard at the gate.
" What is the news, that you ride so late ? "   10
" News most pressing, that must be spoken
To Caesar alone, and that cannot wait."

" The Caesar sleeps ; you must show a token
That the news suffice that he be awoken.
What is the news, and whence do you come ?   15
For no light cause may his sleep be broken."

" Out of the dark of the sands I come,
From the dark of death, with news for Rome.
A word so fell that it must be uttered
Though it strike the soul of the Caesar dumb."   20

Caesar turned in his bed and muttered,
With a struggle for breath the lamp-flame guttered ;
Calpurnia heard her husband moan :
         " The house is falling,
The beaten men come into their own."   25

" Speak your word," said the guard at the gate ;
" Yes, but bear it to Caesar straight,
Say, ' Your murderer's knives are honing,
Your killer's gang is lying in wait.'

" Out of the wind that is blowing and moaning, 30
Through the city palace and the country loaning,
I cry, ' For the world's sake, Caesar, beware,
And take this warning as my atoning.

" ' Beware of the Court, of the palace stair,
Of the downcast friend who speaks so fair, 35
Keep from the Senate, for Death is going
On many men's feet to meet you there.'

" I, who am dead, have ways of knowing
Of the crop of death that the quick are sowing.
I, who was Pompey, cry it aloud 40
From the dark of death, from the wind blowing.

" I, who was Pompey, once was proud,
Now I lie in the sand without a shroud ;
I cry to Caesar out of my pain,
' Caesar, beware, your death is vowed.' " 45

The light grew grey on the window-pane,
The windcocks swung in a burst of rain,
The window of Caesar flung unshuttered,
The horse-hoofs died into wind again.

Caesar turned in his bed and muttered, 50
With a struggle for breath the lamp-flame guttered ;
Calpurnia heard her husband moan :
    " The house is falling,
The beaten men come into their own."

JOHN MASEFIELD
(*20th Century*)

KIRKBRIDE

Bury me in Kirkbride
  Where the Lord's redeem'd anes lie !
The auld kirkyard on the grey hillside
      Under the open sky ;
      Under the open sky,
  On the briest o' the braes sae steep
And side by side wi' the banes that lie
  Streikit there in their hin-maist sleep.
This puir dune body maun sune be dust,
  But it thrills wi' a stoun' o' pride
To ken it may mix with the great and just
  That slumber in thee, Kirkbride.

Little o' peace or rest
  Had we, that hae aften stude
Wi' oor face to the foe on the mountain crest,
      Sheddin' oor dear heart's blude ;
      Sheddin' oor dear heart's blude
  For the rights that the Covenant claimed,
And ready wi' life to mak language guid
  Gin the King or his kirk we blam'd ;
And aften I thocht in the dismal day
  We'd never see gloamin' tide,
But melt like the cranreuch's rime that lay
  In the dawin' abune Kirkbride.

But gloamin' fa's at last
  On the dour, dreich, dinsome day,
And the trouble through whilk we hae safely past
      Has left us weary and wae ;
      Has left us weary and wae,
  And fain to be laid limb-free ;

streikit : *stretched*	dreich : *dreary*
cranreuch : *hoar frost*	dinsome : *full of noise*

Line numbers in right margin: 5, 10, 15, 20, 25, 30

In a dreamless dwaum to be airted away
    To the shores o' the crystal sea ;
Far frae the toil, and the moil, and the mirk,
    And the tyrant's cursed pride—
Row'd in a wreath o' the mists that lurk,   35
    Heaven-sent, aboot auld Kirkbride.

Wheesht ! did the saft win' speak ?
    Or a yaumerin' nicht bird cry ?
Did I dream that a warm haun touch't my cheek,
        And a winsome face gaed by ?   40
        And a winsome face gaed by,
    Wi' a far-aff licht in its e'en—
A licht that bude come frae the dazzling sky,
    For it spak' o' the starnie's sheen.
Age may be donar't, and dazed, and blin',   45
    But I'se warrant, whate'er betide,
A true heart there may tryst wi' my ain,
    And the tryst-word seem'd " Kirkbride."

Hark ! frae the far hilltops,
    And laich frae the lanesome glen,   50
Some sweet psalm tune, like a late dew, drops
        Its wild notes doon the win' ;
        Its wild notes doon the win',
    Wi' a kent soun' owre my min',
For we sang't on the muir—a wheen huntit men—   55
    Wi' oor lives in oor haun langsyne ;
But never a voice can disturb this sang
    Were it Claver'se in a' his pride,
For it's raised by the Lord's ain ransomed thrang
    Forgethered abune Kirkbride.   60

dwaum : *swoon*   donart : *stupid*

airted : *guided*   laich : *low*

yaumerin' : *crying*   wheen : *small number*

bude come : *must have come*   forgethered : *met together*

I hear May Moril's tongue
  That I wistna to hear again,
And there—'twas the black M'Michael's rung
      Clear in the closin' strain ;
      Clear in the closin' strain,   65
  Frae his big heart bauld and true ;
It stirs my saul as in days bygane,
  When his guid braid-sword he drew ;
I needs be aff to the muirs aince mair,
  For he'll miss me by his side ;   70
I' the thrang o' the battle I aye was there,
  And sae maun it be in Kirkbride.

Rax me my staff and plaid,
  That in readiness I may be,
And dinna forget that the Book be laid   75
      Open across my knee ;
      Open across my knee,
  And a text close by my thoom.
And tell me true, for I scarce can see,
  That the words are " Lo ! I come ; "   80
Then carry me through at the Cample ford,
  And up at the lang hillside,
And I'll wait the comin' o' God the Lord
  In a neuk o' the auld Kirkbride.

ROBERT REID

thrang : *press*   rax : *reach*

REQUIEM

Under the wide and starry sky,
Dig the grave and let me lie.
Glad did I live and gladly die,
    And I laid me down with a will.

This be the verse you grave for me :
Here he lies where he longed to be ;
Home is the sailor, home from sea,
    And the hunter home from the hill.

R. L. STEVENSON
(1850-1894)

EVEN SUCH IS TIME

Even such is Time, that takes in trust
Our youth, our joys, our all we have,
And pays us but with earth and dust ;
Who in the dark and silent grave,
When we have wander'd all our ways,
Shuts up the story of our days.
But from this earth, this grave, this dust,
My God shall raise me up, I trust.

RALEIGH
(1552-1618)

NOTES ON THE POEMS

The numbers in brackets after the titles refer to the pages in the text on which the poems appear.

PRACTICE IN RHYTHM (13)

1. We read extract III at the greatest speed and extract I most slowly.

2. Poetry is of all language the most musical, and music must be heard. But the music has a meaning and we must hear the right meaning. In extract I, the solemn majesty of the Angel of Death suggests dignity, not speed. In extract II, the mare trotted at the beginning and galloped at the close, but not at all with the breathless speed of extract III.

As a further illustration take the following pairs of metres :

$$
\begin{array}{ll}
(a) & /\,\smile\,\smile \mid /\,\smile\,\smile \mid /\,\smile\,\smile \mid /\,\smile\,\smile \mid \\
(b) & \smile\,\smile\,/ \mid \smile\,\smile\,/ \mid \smile\,\smile\,/ \mid \smile\,\smile\,/ \mid \\
(c) & /\,\smile\,\smile\,\smile \mid\mid /\,\smile\,\smile\,\smile \mid\mid /\,\smile\,\smile\,\smile \mid\mid /\,\smile\,\smile \mid \\
(d) & \smile\,\smile\,/ \mid\mid \smile\,\smile\,\smile\,/ \mid \smile\,\smile\,\smile\,/ \mid \smile\,\smile\,\smile\,/ \mid
\end{array}
$$

You will notice that the first in each pair is just the second read backwards. But which rhythm in each pair goes the faster ?

This question of course is absurd, as neither rhythm " goes " at all, nor can " go ", until words are put to it.

Now try the lines :

(a)   1. *Lock the door, Lariston, Lion of Liddesdale*

(b)
    2. *But the Angel of Death spread his wings on the blast*
    3. *Did you hear of the curate who mounted his mare*
    4. *Till at length into Aix Roland galloped and stood*

Here 1 is surely faster than 2 and probably faster, certainly fiercer than 3, but as to 4 I leave you to decide.

Compare again, for the second pair of rhythms :

(c)   *Who shall put a bridle on the mourner's lips to chasten them*

(d)   *It was morning at St. Helen's in the great and gallant days*

Here (d) is brighter, gayer, faster than (c).

We may conclude then that the speed and manner of our reading depends not on the metre, but on the poem itself.

3. **That** you might feel the effect of the broken rhythm in **the** last line. Read the limerick aloud and see what you can make of this line.

4. The answer is given in the last sentence of note 2, (page 209).
In this book rhythm will mean the movement of a line of poetry.
When we talk of the movement of a river, we do not mean that there are two things, a movement and a river, but one thing, a moving river. When we talk of the graceful dancing of a girl, we do not mean that there are two things, a graceful dancing and **a** girl, but one, a girl dancing gracefully. So, when we talk of the rhythm of a line of poetry, there are not two things, a rhythm and a line of poetry, but one thing, a rhythmical line of poetry. We may say quite correctly that a rhythm gallops as in extract III, or trots **as** in extract II, or moves with **slow** dignity as in extract I, so long as we remember that what we **mean is** that the line or poem gallops, or trots, or moves with slow dignity.

5. Professor Thomson talks of the instinct for rhythm and Professor Abercrombie of the instinctive pleasure we take in it. This means that the feeling for rhythm is born in us. If, when you are walking along a street, a band strikes up a march, you tend at once to fall into step. Why? Because otherwise you are walking one rhythm and hearing another, and you cannot shut your ears to the band. It is much easier to keep time to the band, march with the music, and so the two rhythms, that of your walking and that of the band, become one. You do not need to think about it : you find yourself doing it. Why do we require music to dance to ? Because a dance is a rhythmical movement, but we must all keep to the same rhythm. This the music gives to us all. Though you had never heard the music before, you would be able to tell at once whether it was a waltz or a Highland Schottische. How ? By the rhythm. Thus when we read poetry aloud we may be attending to the thought expressed, but at the same time we feel the rhythm, without knowing it, and it appears in the manner in which we read. Sometimes, even when the thought is absurd, we find ourselves enchanted with the rhythm. Take these two dancing lines and read them lightly :

James James Morrison Morrison Wetherby George Dupree,
Took great care of his Mother though he was only three.

This is part of the magic of poetry, that, through its rhythm, it appeals to something in us that is deeper than thought, something that no one can explain, and so we call it an instinct.

*   *   *

1. The usual place is at the end of the line ; sometimes we find it in the middle of the line ; rarely anywhere else.

2. The effect is to make it ring more clearly. Because it has its regular place in the rhythm, we look for it, expect it, hear it more clearly. Thus the rhyme depends for its effect on the rhythm.

I have often found in prose, though not by the ear, a word resembling another word in sound ; somehow I did not seem to hear them.

> *In prose as you know I often have found,*
> *Though strange to say it was not by the ear,*
> *One word resembling another in sound,*
> *For them I confess I did not hear.*

You hear them now, don't you ? These same two rhymes are in the prose sentence above. Did you notice them before they were given their position in the rhythm of the doggerel ?

3. In this passage the rhyme is markedly affected by the rhythm. Here is the rhythm scheme with the rhyme attached :

$$| \; / \; \smile \; | \quad / \; | \; \smile \; \acute{\text{deep}}$$
$$| \; \smile \; / \; | \; \smile \; / \; | \; \smile \; / \; | \; \smile \; \acute{\text{creep}}$$
$$| \; / \; \smile \; | \; \smile \; / \; | \; \smile \; / \; | \; \smile \; / \; | \; \smile \; \acute{\text{weep}}$$
$$| \; / \; \smile \; | \; \smile \; / \; | \; \smile \; / \; | \; \smile \; / \; | \; \smile \; / \; | \; \smile \; \acute{\text{sleep.}}$$

In each line, after the first, we have to wait one foot longer for the rhyming word for which our ear is listening, and this delay arouses expectancy, and seems to double our pleasure in the rhyming word when it does come. This effect is entirely lost in the changed version. The rhymes seem almost to have become commonplace. *In fact, the rhymes have lost their magic, because we have changed the rhythm.*

4. Read this changed version carefully and you will find that, though the last line still ends in "sleep", somehow it is not the same "sleep", as expectancy has not been aroused ; and this has clearly affected the rhythm. It may be true to say that the rhythm is in form the same as the original, but in fact something has gone from it that made us hang upon each foot—the expectancy roused by the rhyme. Read it again and you will see that it has become almost commonplace. *In fact, the rhythm has lost its magic, because we have changed the rhyme.*

You must decide. Which version keeps more closely to the original ?

5.

1. At first glance it seems to be *a a b b.* But you must never trust the eye for rhyme. Rhyme must be heard. Read the passage aloud and you will hear that there is middle rhyme as well as end rhyme. The rhythm and rhyme scheme would go thus :

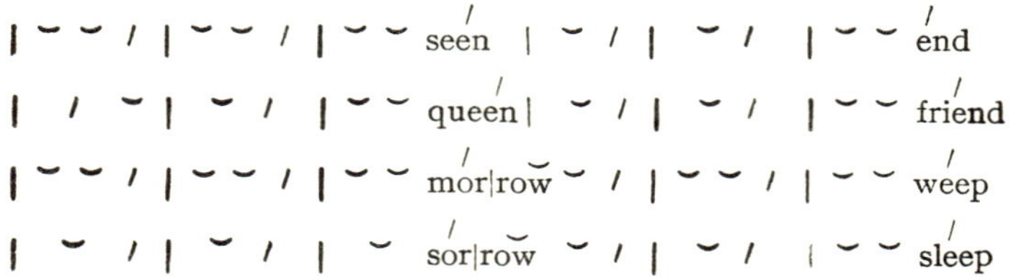

| ˘ ˘ / | ˘ ˘ / | ˘ ˘ seén | ˘ / | ˘ / | ˘ ˘ énd
| / ˘ | ˘ / | ˘ ˘ queén | ˘ / | ˘ / | ˘ ˘ friénd
| ˘ ˘ / | ˘ ˘ / | ˘ ˘ mór|row ˘ / | ˘ ˘ / | ˘ ˘ weép
| ˘ / | ˘ / | ˘ sór|row ˘ / | ˘ / | ˘ ˘ sleép

so that the rhyme scheme is *a b a b c d c d,* as if the passage consisted of eight short lines each of three feet.

2. See answers 3 and 4 (page 211), especially the last sentence of each. Note that by changing the two words we lose the beautiful sound of the middle rhyme, and so four words, one in each line, are heard with far less clarity, *e.g.* the word " queen " in line 2 no longer chimes to the memory of the word " seen ". But we have not only lost the music of the middle rhyme, but that place in the line has lost its importance, and the six feet flow unperturbed to the end of each line. Thus the effect of the rhythm is also changed, some of its magic lost.

3. There is a natural pause, however short, at the end of each line for the sake of the rhythm. In line 1 of the original there is neither the need nor the wish for a pause at " seen ", but if the line were split into two, " seen " would be at the end of the first short line, and a pause would be thrust upon us. Again, see the rhythm and rhyme scheme in note 1, above. Note that, in lines 3 and 4, the words " morrow " and " sorrow " carry us over from the 3rd foot into the fourth, as the first syllable in each of these words forms the strong accent in the 3rd foot, while the second syllable forms the first weak accent in the 4th foot. This would be lost if we split the lines. Read the eight lines as given in question 3 and you will find that you tend to read them faster, and that there is a jerky effect which was not in the original. There is a dignity in the long rolling line and a richness in its hidden middle rhyme that are entirely lost if we split the lines.

✱　　✱　　✱

I

1. One thing has been taken at a time that each might be simpler. In Practice in Rhythm, we saw (note 2, page 209) that we could not separate rhythm from the poem itself ; then in Practice in Rhyme (see especially questions 3 and 4, page 17, and the notes, page 211) that rhythm and rhyme could not be separated. You can no more separate rhythm and rhyme from the poem itself than you can separate the taste and the scent of an orange from the orange.

2. Surely we are dancing. The rhythm tells us. If the poem went thus :

> *From woods and glens*
> *We come, we come,*
> *From isles in streams,*
> *Where waves are dumb,*

we might be walking or marching. Mr. Abercrombie says of this poem, " Its metre sings itself irresistibly into our minds." It not only sings, but dances itself into my mind.

3. As I read these lines there are four strong accents in them, with a beat of silence after the word " listening ". I imagine it a line with five beats, but the second one silent, thus :

| Listening | ' | to my | sweet | pipings |

Note how effective the beat of silence is, coming where it does in the line. Note also that lines 6-10 have three beats each, and go rather fast. But line 11 has four beats and thus delays us with its extra beat—and then comes

Listening   ' to my   sweet   pipings.

4. In the first place, there is the rhyme. The scheme is *a b a b c d e d e f f c*, with double rhymes at *a,a*, *c,c*, and *d,d*.
But rhyme is only one form of the sound music which poets use, and, as we shall see later, they sometimes dispense with it altogether. In fact, much of our greatest poetry is written in blank verse.
Secondly, there are the repetitions, in line 2 and lines 5 and 12. You may have learned from Book III the importance, both for sound and meaning, of repetition in poetry.
Thirdly, there is the alliteration : in line 6, " reeds ", " rushes " ; in line 7, " bees ", " bells " ; in line 8, " birds ", " bushes ".
Fourthly, you know how effective a pause of silence is in music. We have such a pause in lines 5 and 12.

II

1. The stanza may be read thus :

Lines	1 and 2,	.	6 strong beats.	
,,	3 and 4,	.	3	,, ,,
,,	5 and 6,	.	5	,, ,,
Line	7, .	.	3	,, ,,
,,	8, .	.	5	,, ,,

2. So far we have dealt with strong and weak accents. But take the first four words of line 1 :

O bold majestic downs.

What accent are we to put over " O " ? It is not strong, certainly not so strong as " bold ", and it is not weak, certainly not so weak as the first syllable in " majestic ". Let us call it medium and mark it thus (/) :

O bold majestic downs.

In line 2 it is quite definitely strong :

O bold majestic downs, smooth, fair and lonely :
O still solitude only matched in the skies.

3.

Perilous in steep places,
Soft in the level races.

The difference is due to the two strong accents coming together in line 3—" steep places ".

4. The rhyme scheme seems to be *a b c c b b d d*. But " only ", in line 2, rhymes with " lonely ", in line 1. Is this merely a chance rhyme or did the poet intend it ? See page 33, where the whole poem is given There you will find that in stanza 2 the word " uprising " in line 2 (occupying the same position in the line as " only ") rhymes with " surprising " in line 1. Similarly, in stanza 3, " dashing " rhymes with " plashing ". So the rhyme scheme is *a a b c c b b d d*. Now re-read the stanza and note how, because of the rhyme, you tend to emphasise " only " and so affect the rhythm.

5. **Line 1.** Note the long vowels in

" O ", " bold ", " downs ", " smooth ", " fair ", " lonely ".

These give a feeling of spaciousness that suits the meaning.
Line 2. Note the alliteration in " still ", " solitude ", " skies ".
For " only " see note 4, above.
Line 3. Note the effect of the sharp consonant " p ", especially in " steep places ". You are forced to pause after " steep " if you are not to say " steeplaces ". Does it not emphasise the feeling of the perilous steep ?

6. Line 5. Again, as in line 1, the long vowels give the feeling of spaciousness so suitable to the meaning—" Where ", " sweeping ", " silence ", " cloud-land ", " flies ".

Line 6. Note how the word " undulation " undulates in accents, strong, weak, strong, weak. Note also the liquid effect of the letter " l ", occurring in four syllables.

Line 7. After line 6, this line seems full of thorns. You cannot read it quickly and pronounce the final sound in " entrenched ", the " th " in " with thickets thorned ".

Line 8. The sound of the three words, " delicate ", " miniature ", " dainty ", suggests the meaning. Compare the effect with that of " bold, majestic downs ".

III

1. From the reeds beside the almost stagnant stream you see the swan rise. Think of its size and the stretch of its wings. You see it climbing or scaling the upward sky, and hear the powerful beat of its strong wings. You watch it high above your head in the sunlight (its bright course) winging its way out over the measureless stretch of the shining sea.

IV

1. If we drop the " the " out of lines 1 and 2 they become statements of ordinary facts, for we are all, to a certain extent, makers of music and dreamers of dreams. But our music and dreams do not move and shake the world. Only the music and dreams of master minds, of great spirits, of *the* music-makers and *the* dreamers of dreams, can do this.

2. It is a poet who speaks, therefore, in a narrow sense " we " means the great poets, but in reality it means the great men of all times, poets, musicians, artists, scientists, philosophers, explorers, etc.
" Makers " here has something of the meaning of " creators "—those who bring forth new things, not merely imitating or copying the past, but making music new to us and leading to the future. Note that " poet " comes from a Greek word which means " to make ", and the old Scots word for a poet is " makar ".

3. We measure the greatness of any man by the effect he has on the world. We all have a certain effect on our own little world of friends, and we can move and shake them, if we do something especially good or bad. Think, then, of Shakespeare and Columbus, and how they have shaken and moved the world.

4. See 3 above. Until they have moved and shaken the world, their real greatness is not recognised, and this rarely happens in their own life-time. And so they lose the world—its glory and its rewards—forsake

it, forget it in their dreams of what should be and what may come to pass in the future through them. A prophet has no honour in his own country, nor in his own age.

5. It is a statement of fact, but in a metaphorical form. How often have the greatest spirits been " despised and rejected of men ". But, in addition, they often need loneliness that they may dream—make their music—undisturbed.
For line 4 of the stanza, compare Psalm 137, verse 1.

6. (*a*) We might divide the stanza into three parts :
1. Lines 1-2 : A statement of who they are.
2.   ,,   3-6 : A statement of their place in the world of their time.
3.   ,,   7-8 : A statement of their effect on the world.

But there are not three statements in the stanza. If there were, we should have to link them together in thought. But, by weaving them into one sentence, the poet makes it impossible for us to stop, even in thought, until we have reached the triumphant conclusion. It is as if the poet said, " This is true, and this is true, and this is true, *yet this is also true* ". Note that line 7 begins with " yet ".
(*b*) The rhyme scheme is *a b a b a b a b*, the same two sounds being repeated alternately, so that to the ear it is a unity of sound, as to the mind it is a unity of thought.

V

1. The effect of music or poetry on us is to lift us, for the time being, above the little things of life, to give wings to our imagination. It is like looking at the sea. Arnold in " Self-dependence " says of the sea :

> *Still, still let me, as I gaze upon you,*
> *Feel my soul becoming vast like you.*

2. The sea-gull represents the singer exalted with the joy of making his music.

3. There are, in both, " the lone sea-breakers " and the same feeling of loneliness and triumphant joy.

✸   ✸   ✸

GLYCINE'S SONG (23)

1. When you have chosen your corner at a picnic and built your fire carefully, you do not expect anything to happen until you apply a match. How is the poem or the picture in the poem to come alive ? The poet has built it carefully. It needs only the fire of your imagination. When we read a poem and say, " Well, I can see nothing in that," the truth generally is that there is nothing in us, no kindling imagination. Apply this to stanza 2. We have the sunny shaft, the bird " poised ", hovering

216

therein, " his eyes of fire, his beak of gold "—think how it would gleam in the sun—"all else of amethyst", *i.e.* violet. "He sank, he rose, he twinkled "—the dictionary gives—" twinkle—to shine, with rapidly pulsating or dancing light, to sparkle ". Think of him hovering, sparkling in the sunlight.

2. The one that remains with me is " that shaft of sunny mist ".

3. See Practice in Rhyme, question II, 3 (page 18) and note II, 3 (page 212). There we lost the dignity of the long rolling line by dividing it into two. Here the effect is just the opposite. The lines represent a bird's song, and the short lines with the pause at the end of each suggest the chirping of the bird. Again I always imagine that the bird is flying away from me, that its song is dying on the air, and the short lines give this suggestion perfectly, the last sound being, " To-day, to-day ".

*   *   *

THE DESTRUCTION OF SENNACHERIB (25)

1. (*a*) In verse 35 he found the facts of the story. But note that the prose gives only the bare facts—the angel of the Lord smote that night in the camp of the Assyrians 185,000 : and when the rest arose early in the morning they found them all dead.

(*b*) Read the whole chapter and you will see that he found there also the splendour and the pride of the Assyrians. This gives us stanza 1, but the spirit runs through the whole poem.

(*c*) It gives us the mystery of the destruction of the Assyrians.

(*d*) It makes us feel the littleness of man matched with the sublimity of God, and gives to Byron's style that solemn dignity which, together with the mystery, forms the atmosphere of the poem.

> *And the might of the Gentile, unsmote by the sword,*
> *Hath melted like snow in the glance of the Lord !*

See also " The Vision of Belshazzar ", Book III, page 192.

2. Here you must choose for yourself. The one that remains most vividly with me is stanza 3.

3. You cannot tell from the poem. But in the prose, verse 33, Isaiah says " By the way that he came, by the same shall he return," and verses 36-7 of the same chapter tell us :

> *So Sennacherib king of Assyria departed, and went and returned, and dwelt at Nineveh.*

> *And it came to pass, as he was worshipping in the house of Nisroch his god, that Adrammelech and Sharezer his sons smote him with the sword : and they escaped into the land of Armenia. And Esarhaddon his son reigned in his stead.*

*   *   *

217

1. Stanzas 1-4 : An atmosphere of alarm, of coming danger.
   „   5-7 : An atmosphere of joy in the coming fight.
   „   8-10 : An atmosphere of battle and the triumph of victory.

2. We might say that one is the reverse of the other. In stanzas 1-3, pages 13-14, the rhythm, with the single variation that the first foot may have two or three syllables, goes thus :

$$|\;\smile\smile\;/\;|\;\smile\smile\;/\;|\;\smile\smile\;/\;|\;\smile\smile\;/\;|$$

As a general rule line 1 of each stanza of this poem goes thus :

$$|\;/\;\smile\smile\;|\;/\;\smile\smile\;|\;/\;\smile\smile\;|\;/\;\smile\smile\;|$$

and lines 2 and 5 thus :

$$|\;/\;\smile\smile\;|\;/\;\smile\smile\;|\;/\;\smile\smile\;|\;/\;\quad|$$

It will be interesting for you to find the variations for yourself.
The poem is to be full of sound, so it begins on the strong accent. Note, too, that generally the alliterated syllables bear the strong accent :

Lock the door, Lariston, Lion of Liddesdale

Fierce is the foray, and far is the cry.

Again it will be interesting to find exceptions. In addition, the poem opens with a cry of alarm, of coming danger. Note how the first line bursts on you like a shout.

3. Because the subject deals with the cry of alarm, the mustering of armies, the battle, the shout of triumph. The words of the poem must not only tell us of this but must sound in harmony with the sense. We must not merely be told about the battle. We must hear it.
In the next poem one person only speaks, and speaks to himself. In this poem we hear the messenger and Jock Elliot speak, and the Scots shout in triumph.

4. The first line of each stanza is unrhymed. The rhymes are generally single. There are a few examples of double rhyme such as "flying ", "crying "; "ranger", "danger "; "foemen ", "no men "; and one example of triple rhyme: "Northumberland ", "Cumberland ".

5. (*a*) Stanzas 5 and 7. It is worth noting that stanzas 5-7 form the quiet part of the poem.
(*b*) Here you must choose for yourself. But stanza 1, line 1 ; stanza 2, line 5 ; and perhaps stanza 9, line 5, are worth considering.

6. **Here again you must find your own.** I give two and leave the rest to you. *" Fierce* is the *foray* ", *" In shivers* were *shorn* "*.

7. First line. The poem opens with a cry of alarm at the coming of the foe·
Last line. The poem closes with a shout of triumph over the defeat of the foe.

8. Instead of taking the messenger's advice and shutting himself in the Breaken tower, Jock Elliot led out his men, defeated the English, and so locked the door to their advance in the most effective way.

✻   ✻   ✻

<u>THE PATRIOT</u> (29)

1. The word " misdeeds ". We should not be sure whether he was confessing that they were misdeeds, or meant that other people called them misdeeds. On this question depends the whole interpretation of the poem

2. The question is answered in stanza 6, lines 3-5. We might paraphrase it thus : " If in my triumph I had dropped down dead, God might have said to me, ' You have been paid by the world for what you did. Now what do you owe me ? ' Now, instead God shall repay me for all I have tried to do in this year. I am safer so." The man who feels thus at the thought of facing God, must feel that he at least has done his best, aimed at the right, though all others condemned him.

3. In stanza 2, he says the people would willingly have given him the sun out of the skies. Here the word is used literally. In stanza 3, line 1, it is used metaphorically for that which is the best in life. He had aimed at that to give it to his loving friends, his compatriots.

4. Because he was a real patriot, a real lover of his people, who aimed at the right, one of the " music-makers " (page 21). Such men, if they are really great, are rarely understood by their contemporaries. Think of Socrates, one of the world's great men, and a great patriot. When condemned to death by the Athenians he would not even think of escape, because as an Athenian he would not evade the laws of his own land. Read also Isaiah LIII, verses 3 and 4.

5. (*a*) See note 4 above.
A year ago he had been the popular hero, he had accomplished something that the people desired greatly. But his ideals, his aims for the city, were too high for the people. They either did not understand them, or, where they did, found that they contradicted their own selfish aims. During the year they found also that they could neither bend him to their will nor could they reach or hurt his spirit. Hence the revulsion in feeling. They hated him all the more, because once they had loved him.
(*b*) You must choose your own line here. It will almost certainly be in stanza 5. The one I choose is stanza 5, line 2.

219

6. See " Lock the Door, Lariston ", note 3 (page 218).
This poem is what is called a dramatic monologue, a poem in which one person speaks at some dramatic moment in his life revealing something of his own character and story.   It resembles the soliloquy in drama, except that in some dramatic monologues the person is speaking to another.
The Patriot is speaking to himself ; we are hearing his thoughts.   There is little need for sound in this poem.   It would lose far less by being read silently than " Lock the Door, Lariston ".

*   *   *

TO THE MUSES (31)

1. Lines 13, 14.

2. In building up this prose sentence we draw :

    (a) from stanza 1 : wheresoever,
    (b) from stanza 2 : ye wander (line 5)
    (c) from stanza 3 : fair Nine (line 12)
    (d) from stanza 4 : ye have so neglected your ancient love for poetry that little is being produced now.

Thus, from the first three stanzas we draw only " wheresoever ye wander, fair Nine ", while all the rest of the sentence comes from stanza 4.

3. By delaying his main statement till the end, Blake keeps us wandering and wondering with his Muses, unhurried, but led on from one beautiful picture to another, unable to stop, because we want to know where the poet is leading us.   Once we know that, we stop, but we do not know it until we reach the end of the poem.

4. We have learned Blake's method of constructing his poem.   Many people are apt to think that a poet just sits down and writes his poem. Some poems may be written in this way.   But no perfect lyric, such as this, can be written without real feeling and real hard work.   Professor Minto has said that a perfect lyric can no more be fashioned out of words without labour than a statue can be carved out of marble.   Suppose Blake had begun with his main statement what would have been the effect on the poem ?   Take the first sentence of Johnson's " Rasselas " :

Ye who listen with credulity to the whispers of fancy, and pursue with eagerness the phantoms of hope, who expect that age will perform the promises of youth and that the deficiencies of the present will be supplied by the morrow, attend to the history of Rasselas, Prince of Abyssinia :

Now note the effect of putting the main statement at the beginning :

Attend to the history of Rasselas, Prince of Abyssinia, ye who listen with credulity to the whispers of fancy, and pursue with eagerness the phantoms of hope, who expect that age will perform the promises of youth and that the deficiencies of the present will be supplied by the morrow.

220

Our finely constructed sentence has become loose and rambling, a main statement dragging after it a tail of subordinate clauses which might be of any length ; for note we might stop at " fancy ", or " hope ", or " youth ", or " morrow ", or there might be two or three more subordinate clauses. There is nothing but the period to tell us we have come to the end. Had Blake begun with the main statement the effect would have been similar. Compare with the next poem.

5. I think perhaps in stanza 2, and especially in the adjectives. Think of Shakespeare's line :

Come unto these yellow sands.

How simple is the one word " yellow ", yet how much it says ! Note then, Blake's " green " corners of the earth, " blue " regions of the air, and " melodious " winds. "Green", "blue", and "melodious" seem to tell us of all the beauties of earth and heaven, and of all the music of the wind.

6. At this time there was little real lyric poetry being produced in England, though Burns was pouring forth a flood of beautiful lyrics in Scotland. But Blake's call brought the Muses back ; for immediately after this, Wordsworth, Scott, Coleridge, and, later, Byron, Shelley, and Keats gave to England her second great period of poetry.

From THE LOTOS-EATERS (32)

2. I do not think so. In note 4 (page 220), you will see the distinction between what are called a periodic and a loose sentence. Tennyson has in two ways definitely prevented us from feeling that the long sentence, lines 1-7, is loose.

(*a*) The first word in lines 5 and 7, " music ", is a reiteration of the word " music " in the principal clause and takes us back to it.
(*b*) The characteristic thing about a loose sentence is that it merely stops, it does not conclude. We know we have come to the end only because of the punctuation mark, the period. But the rhythm of line 7 tells us definitely we have come to the end. Each addition to the sentence contained in lines 1 and 2 takes a couple of lines, *i.e.*, 3 and 4, 5 and 6. The third addition, however, is a single line, longer than the others, a long rolling hexameter, which makes us feel the end even before we see the period. It has the effect of a definite conclusion.

3. I think lines 5 and 6.

*   *   *

2. Yes. They are exactly the same, even to the point that where he uses double-rhyme in stanza 1 he does the same in 2 and 3.
   Thus in 1 we have " lonely ", " only "; " places ", " races ";
     in 2 we have " surprising ", " uprising "; " ascending ", " blending ";
     in 3 we have " plashing ", " dashing "; " veering ", " rearing "
   If we put capitals for double rhymes, and small letters for single, the rhyme scheme of all three stanzas is *A, A, b, C, C, b, b, d, d.*

3. See Practice in Interpretation, note 6 (page 215). The aim of the poet, I think, in line 5 is to give the feeling of spaciousness, and this is helped at once by the change in rhythm. After the two short lines, the long pentameter conveys a sense of freedom and sweeping ease.

4. When you stand on a cliff and look down on the sea beneath, you feel your height above. But if you let your eye travel out to the distant horizon, to the line where sky and sea meet, you feel that it is on a level with you. The sea seems to rise up to your level as if it were a rising plain or hill. Hence the sight surprising,

   Of sea in front uprising, steep and wide.

   Hence the ships sailing away from you seem to be ascending to heaven. The distance is so great that they seem very small, and hardly to be moving at all.
   But there is something else surprising. Imagine that you are walking across the downs, seeing all the sights described in stanza 1. You " climb the crown, and lo ! " the sea and all the sights of the second stanza appear suddenly before you.

5. Line 16. See note 4 above.
   This is the longest line in the poem. It has the largest number of words in it, eleven, and of these nine are monosyllables, all, except one, of two, three, or four letters. We feel the line long, drawn out. Note the effect also of dropping out the word " would ". The line would then mean that the ships were pointing the way they were going. But as it is, it suggests that they are only " wearily pointing the way " they would like to go. This effect is emphasized by the alliteration, " wearily ", " would ". Read the line slowly, noting the number of little words, and you will feel as if the rhythm tottered and dragged its way along.
   Line 17. Here we have the effect of the words " murmur " and " plashing ", the sounds of which suggest their meaning. Such words are called onomatopoeic, because the sound " makes the name " or suggests the word.

6. Think of the effects produced by the rhythm, the rhyme, and the careful choice of words, and you will have some idea of how much care and thought and real hard work are necessary for the composition of such a poem. Add to that the poetic inspiration which gave it birth, and which guided and governed all.
   The next poem is a wonderful contrast in style.

1. Line 1 has three beats or accented syllables; lines 2, 3, and 4 have two each. This is not what we should expect from their appearance on the page. But line 1 consists of six syllables, lines 2 and 3 of three syllables, and line 4 of five syllables; in addition, lines 1, 2, and 3 begin each with a strong beat and line 4 with a weak beat. Note the quaint effect of the rhythm:

> *Welcome, maids of honour !*
> *You do bring*
> *In the spring,*
> *And wait upon her.*

2. I: Welcome, honour, upon.   II: Virgins, many, any.
III: Maidens, posies, damask, roses.   IV: Respected, neglected.
All the other words, forty-two, are monosyllables.
You cannot fail to see how simple the language of the poem is.

3. Yes. It is a short, little poem, absolutely simple—simple in language · simple in grammar: simple in thought: simple in rhyme scheme (every stanza the same, *i.e.*, *a b b a* and the "*a*" rhymes double): simple and quaint in rhythm (again every stanza the same), the whole effect one of infinite sweetness and beauty. And can anything be more sweet or more beautiful than the violet ?

In the first line the violets are called maids of honour. The spring, then, is a queen or princess, and the violets the most honoured of her attendants. Of all the flowers of spring, in that single phrase Herrick puts the violets first. Think of the almost stark simplicity of the last stanza. It says, " Though you are thus respected, afterwards you lie neglected." It is quite true, but is it not almost commonplace ? This is the danger of the simple style. Herrick, however, in one phrase, brings into this statement all the sweetness, the delicacy, the beauty of the violets. In the last line he calls them " poor girls ". Had he said " poor flowers ", it would have remained commonplace. But " poor girls " takes us back to the " maids of honour ", no longer honoured, but neglected, and so, " poor girls ".

5. This may seem an absurd question, as we could not write either poem. But when we examine " The Downs " we begin to feel that we understand how Bridges does it; for example, how he gets his effects of rhyme and rhythm, how he makes the sound fit the sense. When we examine " To Violets ", however, it becomes simpler and simpler, so simple that anyone might write it, and yet so sweet and delicate that no one could write it. " The Downs " seems to me a wonderful piece of art, " To Violets " a miracle, like the violet itself. Wotton's stanza is worth reading here:

> *You violets that first appear,*
> *By your pure purple mantles known*
> *Like the proud virgins of the year,*
> *As if the spring were all your own,*
> *What are you, when the rose is blown ?*

1. (*a*) It is a simple tragic tale as many ballads are.
   (*b*) It is simply told, without any touch of adornment.
   (*c*) The poet assumes that we know the story already. He does not tell us why the girls " biggit the bower " ; he assumes that we know the plague was raging in the burrows-town and that they left the town to escape it. Again he says " yon burn-brae " and " their noble kin ", as if we must all know the place and who the girls are.
   (*d*) It has that accent of simple sincerity, of absolute truth, to be found only, we might say, among the best of the old ballads, when the poet is telling what he feels is a true story, a story known to his audience.
   (*c*) It is written in what is called the ballad metre. See " Sir Patrick Spens " (Book III, page 57).

2. When a man is writing a story in prose or verse, his chief aim is to make it sound real, to attend to details and descriptions, to use the right language, so that we may accept it as true, at least for the time being. But in the old ballads the facts of the story are already known. The poet does not try to make us believe in the truth of the story. We know it is true. Why then tell it ? Because something in the story seems so tragic or so beautiful to the poet that he wants everyone to see it. He does not worry about the details, but we see these " twa bonnie lasses " who left the town to escape the plague, see, too, the beauty of the picture of their building their bower, and feel the strangeness of the terrible fate that overtook them. The pest followed and slew them, so that they could not even be buried where they had hoped to lie, among their noble kin, but had to be left " to beik fornent the sin ". And if you had said to the poet that this fate might have happened to any one, I think he would have said as he does at the end of the poem, " Yes, but these were twa bonnie lasses."   It is almost as if he were saying to life, " Why had this to happen to twa innocent bonnie lasses ? " The beauty of this poem is in its simple sincerity and its pathos. It is like a piece of pure gold. Any adornment would spoil it.

3. The fourth stanza is a repetition of the first stanza, but when we reach it we know the whole tragic tale, and it comes with deeper meaning. The first stanza is read brightly and with interest, the fourth meditatively, wonderingly ; and, because no question is asked, we seem to feel the question implied all the more. Compare the effect of this stanza with that of the last stanza of " Sir Patrick Spens " (Book III, page 176) and the wonderful effect of the repetition of " How are the mighty fallen ! " in David's lament for Jonathan. (Book III, page 193). In the same way, this stanza lifts us above the sadness of the story and makes us feel the beauty and mystery of it.

In every way except in rhythm. With this exception all that is said regarding " Bessie Bell and Mary Gray " in notes 1, 2 and 3 applies equally here, even to the repetition of a stanza and its effect on us. Note this difference. In this poem it is stanza 2 that is repeated in the last two stanzas, but in its repetition it is amplified. In stanza 5 we again see him ride out, but more gallantly and more alive—

> *A plume in his helmet,*
> *A sword at his knee,*

and in stanza 6 we again see the riderless horse come home, but there is one terribly significant detail added :

> *Toom cam his saddle*
> *All bloody to see.*

2. The preceding poem moves steadily, slowly, almost meditatively, with little variation. There is a swing and go in the first stanza of this poem like the galloping of Bonnie George Campbell's horse. The pace slows down after line 6. Read stanza 2 and note how spirited the first two lines are, and how fateful the last two.

3. Is it his wife, or the spirit of the dead man, mourning over all he has left ?

*   *   *

THE LAMENT OF THE BORDER WIDOW (38)

1. If you are to understand the full significance of the word " extremitie " you must think of her position. She is left with the dead body of her knight. All his goods have been taken, her servants have all fled. She is absolutely alone, " No living creature came that way ".

2. (*a*) The facts themselves. This woman's love rises above the " extremitie ". Think of her carrying on her back the dead body of the man she loved, sitting down at times exhausted, then staggering on again, digging the grave and laying him in it. Is this not " extremitie " ?
(*b*) Line 20, the words " happed " and " sae green ".
Suppose the line had run " And cover'd him with earth and sod ", we should have lost the tenderness in the word " happed ", as of a mother covering her sleeping baby ; lost, too, the yearning note in " sae green ".

3. (*a*)
> *But think na ye my heart was sair,*
> *When I laid the moul' on his yellow hair.*

(*b*) When the " extremitie " was over. While still she had something to do for him, she had something to live for ; but when it was all finished,
> *O think na ye my heart was wae,*
> *When I turn'd about, away to gae ?*

Now she had nothing left but her memories, and her love which would be faithful to the last.

225

4. (*a*) This statement is true. Only when a woman is tried to the uttermost as in this poem, can we know what she can bear without breaking, only when she is in " extremitie " can we see her true greatness.
(*b*) This statement is also true. If the Border Widow had been a woman of weaker character her actions would have been different, and the story, therefore, different. The story is really the outcome of the character, is just the character in action.

5. The name of the poem would seem to answer the question, but if it were merely sad it would not be a poem. In " The Lament of the Border Widow " we see how the trials of her life bring out her greatness of character. Is this sad ? If we think of her we cannot but admire her. But when we read the poem we *are* her, live her life, face her " extremitie ", and find in ourselves the strength and love to rise above it. This is an uplifting, an ennobling experience.

*   *   *

HELEN OF KIRKCONNEL (40)

1. Stanza 1. Lines 1-2. These state the main theme of the poem, while lines 3-4 repeat it.
Stanza 7. Lines 1-2 practically repeat those of stanza 1 and emphasise the main theme which might well have been forgotten after the passion of stanzas 3-5. Lines 3-4 show how insistent is the call. There is a pathetic eagerness in such words as " bids " and " haste " that makes us feel they are spoken not by the imagination of the poet, but by Helen herself.

Stanza 10. Lines 1-2 repeat those of stanza 1 and bring us back to the main theme at the close of the poem, while lines 3-4 express that utter weariness of life which, growing through the whole poem, culminates in

And I am weary of the skies.

2. We have made both stanzas rather ordinary by dropping one line in each.

None but my foe to be my guide

is a statement of a very significant fact in the story, but when repeated, as in the stanza, there is added a note of exultation and menace that bodes ill for his foe. In stanza 5 the line

I hackéd him in pieces sma

expresses the feeling of vengeance let loose, with a stark simplicity that makes it one of the most appalling lines in literature. But when it is repeated as in the stanza, it gives a feeling not only of vengeance let loose, but of vengeance glutted in a frenzy of hate.

226

the poem stopped at stanza 5, it would be a story of a wrong done
and of the fierce vengeance taken on the offender. But there is some-
thing entirely sweet and beautiful in the love that speaks in stanza 6,
coming as it does after the fires of Hell that burn in stanza 5. As we
read on, we feel that the meaning of the poem is love, not hate,
that the hate springs from wronged love, and, once glutted, is almost
forgotten in the passion that burns like a fever. The last stanzas remind
us of the restless tossing and moaning of one in pain, one who cries for
death as the only cure for his suffering.

4. The story resembles that of the Border Widow in that in each, one of
the lovers is slain and the other, constant in love, is left to mourn. The
following lines are very similar.

Oh think na ye my heart was sair. " Helen of Kirkconnel."

But think na ye my heart was sair. " Border Widow ".

I'll mak a garland o' thy hair " Helen of Kirkconnel ".
Shall bind my heart for evermair
Until the day I die !

Wi' ae lock of his yellow hair " Border Widow ".
I'll chain my heart for evermair.

There is nothing in the Border Widow's experience to correspond to the
fierce satisfaction of Helen's lover (stanzas 4-5). But she has attained
a peace of mind by carrying through the last rites for her knight, a
peace that springs from strength of character and love that has endured
to the uttermost. She is stronger, he more passionate.

5. It is certainly a sad poem, as is " The Lament of the Border Widow ".
The question is repeated here to emphasise the point that it is not merely
sad, or it would not be a poem. Did you enjoy the poem ? If not, it
is not a poem for you. If you did enjoy it, what did you enjoy in it ?
It was not just the sadness. See note 6 to " Edward, Edward " (page
229).

* * *

EDWARD, EDWARD (42)

1. She could not rest till she had confirmation.

2. Note the following points :

(*a*) She rejects at once Edward's first and second answers and still
pushes her question.

227

(*b*) She expresses no sorrow, not even surprise, when she hears of the death of her husband.

(*c*) She proceeds to ask four questions :

1. *And whatten penance will ye dree for that ?*
2. *And what will ye do wi' your towers and your ha' ?*
3. *And what will ye leave to your bairns and your wife ?*
4. *And what will ye leave to your ain mither dear ?*

There is no attempt to console or sympathise with her son, though he is heart-broken and almost beside himself with horror at what he has done.   If the third question had been " And what will ye leave to your *dear* bairns and wife ? " we might have credited her with some feeling, but it is only in the fourth question, where she speaks of herself, that the endearing terms come in.   Look at them again :

> *And what will ye leave to your* ain *mither* dear,
>   *Edward, Edward ;*
> *And what will ye leave to your* ain *mither* dear,
>   *My* dear *son, now tell me, O ?*

(*d*) Edward's reply :

> *The curse of hell frae me shall ye bear ;*
>   *Sic counsels ye gave to me, O !*

As for her character you must form your own opinion of it.   In some points we shall all agree.   She has dominated her son with her evil counsel. She is heartless, scheming, selfish, persistent.   For myself, I do not see her as a stern, commanding woman, but a self-satisfied, sly, demure, insistent serpent of a woman, who pushes her point quietly, steadily, cunningly, and merits entirely the blast of hate with which the poem closes.

3. He dare not confess it even to himself.   Twice he tries to put her off though he knows that she already knows the truth.   Only when she persists with her question does the truth burst from him.

4. His horror and remorse are such that he feels that his own guilt hangs over everything he possesses, that everything should do penance.   Let his towers and hall go to ruin, his wife and children beg through life.

5. The sixth line in each stanza, the words " Mither, mither ".   In stanzas 1 and 2 where he is trying to put her off, the words are spoken in a hesitating, furtive way.

In stanza 3 where the terrible truth bursts from him, they are spoken in an agony of appeal, as if he said, " You have led me to this.   Help me. What am I to do ? "

After that, as her character grows clearer and he realises how entirely she is leaving him to bear the whole responsibility of what he has done, the words grow colder and harder, until in the last stanza where she shows that she is thinking only of herself, they sound like the hiss of hate.

6. This poem consists of a conversation between a mother and her son. It lasts for about three minutes. To read it is an adventure in life. We live these terrible moments. We are no longer ourselves, but Edward, dazed with what he has done, realising what his mother is and what she has led him to, overwhelmed with remorse for the father he loves and has slain, ready to flee from all he has loved and known, to try to lose himself in life. To be for a time the Border Widow, the lover of Helen of Kirkconnel, or Edward, is an experience, an adventure into a new life where we meet remorse and hate and death, and love that conquers and sweetens all. The experience may have its sad or even terrifying side; but who would miss it?

*　　*　　*

THE OLD CLOAK (45)

1. In the last poem we had neither introduction, nor any suggestion of a conclusion, just the short, tense scene. Here we have both introduction and conclusion, each spoken by the husband. In lines 1-4 he tells us the time of the year and the kind of weather—the background to the poem. In lines 5-6 he introduces his wife, and indirectly introduces himself. In the last stanza he repeats line 5, adding, however, a line that casts a humorous light upon it, moralises a bit to cover the fact that he is giving in, and concludes by agreeing to do as she wishes. We feel we have come to the end we expected from the beginning, the end that will probably come to all debates between these two.

2. She says to him:

> " *Rise up, and save cow Crumbock's life.*
> *Man, put thine old cloak about thee!* "

He at once declares he needs a new cloak, and his intention to get one the next day. What about cow Crumbock? Is she to wait till the next day? They argue out the question of the new cloak, apparently without a thought of cow Crumbock. Was he just lazy and unwilling to go, making excuses to put off time? You will notice how quiet and persistent she is without ever beginning to scold. Did she know her husband, know that he would give in at the end? He at any rate knows her:

> " *Yet she will lead me if she can   . . .*
> *It's not for a man with a woman to threap*
> *Unless he first give over the plea.*"

But the whole atmosphere is kindly. There is no touch of bitterness. We smile at this little human comedy and like both the actors.

229

1. No. See lines 17-18. See also the manner of her replies, her assurance, and her triumphant last remark, line 40, when she turns tne tables on him.

2. " Bauld and bricht " (line 17).

*   *   *

THE FAUSE KNICHT UPON THE ROAD (50)

1. I think naturally he would be startled and afraid. At least, he is not like the lady who " tarried for words wi' this stranger knicht ". But he had the courage to face him and reply.

2. When we read the first stanza, remembering who the " fause knicht " is, we cannot help feeling how " wee " the boy is when he replies ; but before we have time to wonder what he will do, come the words " and still he stood ". Then follows question after question, but every question is answered by the wee boy, and after each answer comes " and still he stood " until we feel that nothing could shake him.

3. In the first poem the lady was so far from being afraid that she tarried to talk with the knight. If she replied to each question as it was asked the poem would go thus :

> *O what is higher nor the tree ?*
> *O heaven is higher nor the tree.*
>
> *And what is deeper nor the sea ?*
> *And hell is deeper nor the sea.*
>
> *Or what is heavier nor the lead ?*
> *O sin is heavier nor the lead.*
>
> *And what is better nor the bread ?*
> *The blessing's better nor the bread.*

Each answer comes so pat that our confidence in the lady would never be shaken and we should lose interest. But as question after question is piled one on top of the other in lines 21-30, we begin to wonder if anyone could reply to them, and so begin to fear for her. Accordingly, when she begins to reply, and in six out of her ten replies makes a definite thrust at the character of the knight, our joy in her triumph is increased, and our interest is held to the very end.

On the other hand, we have no such confidence in the wee boy, and his immediate response to the first question encourages us. Stanza by stanza he grows more confident, and we with him, until in the fifth stanza when he jeers at the knight we cannot help laughing at his reply, " A' they that hae blue tails ". It seems, too, that his reply angers the fause knicht, for he ceases to question the wee boy, and instead,

230

begins to wish him evil. But the wee boy has now grown quite sure of himself and is ready for anything the fause knicht may say. To the end, " still he stood ".

Thus each method is " the better ".

4. I should say this poem was the earlier. In the preceding poem we have an introduction which leads up to the debate between the knight and the lady, and a stanza to conclude. There is more art in the construction, the tale is told in a more leisurely fashion. In this poem we begin abruptly and finish as abruptly.

5. This poem always seems to me more real. The preceding poem is like a well-constructed, well-told tale. This one has something of the abruptness and breathlessness of a real experience.

6. Here you must choose for yourself.

JENNY KISSED ME, and DON'T ASK FOR A KISS (52)

1. You will observe in the first poem the real kindliness touched with humour, in the second the humour touched with truth, in both the neatness and dexterity of the workmanship.

2. Following the suggestions in the question, we write it out in form A Now we have only three lines to fill in, and we know that lines 3 and 5 are to rhyme with " sore ", and line 6 with " hurry ". Our final version may be something like form B.

<table>
<tr><td colspan="2" align="center">A.</td><td align="center">B.</td></tr>
<tr><td>1.</td><td>My ankle is sore,</td><td>My ankle is sore,</td></tr>
<tr><td>2.</td><td>So I don't want to hurry.</td><td>So I don't want to hurry.</td></tr>
<tr><td>3.</td><td></td><td>I have told you before</td></tr>
<tr><td>4.</td><td>My ankle is sore.</td><td>My ankle is sore ;</td></tr>
<tr><td>5.</td><td></td><td>So there's no need to roar</td></tr>
<tr><td>6.</td><td></td><td>And get into a flurry.</td></tr>
<tr><td>7.</td><td>My ankle is sore,</td><td>My ankle is sore,</td></tr>
<tr><td>8.</td><td>So I don't want to hurry.</td><td>So I don't want to hurry.</td></tr>
</table>

Do you see how effective the repetition is ? There would not be much left for the brother to say, would there ? Suppose he began :

Your ankle is sore,
When you don't want to hurry.

Could you finish it ?

1. The punctuation shows that these two stanzas consist of a series of questions, one after another, so that the note of interrogation is in our voice all the time.

2. This stanza begins with a command. The poet is done with questions, and the note of interrogation gives place to a more peremptory tone.

3. Yes. We have changed the whole tone of the stanza. Drop lines 2 and 5, and we are left with a stanza of three lines, consisting of two questions, the second of which is a rhetorical question, *i.e.*, one which needs no answer as the answer is so evident. It is almost like a statement, and is here more emphatic. There is even a note of comic impatience in these rhetorical questions :

> *Will, when looking well can't move her,*
> *Looking ill prevail?*
> *Will, when speaking well can't win her,*
> *Saying nothing do't?*

Now the poet is evidently impatient with the lover and this impatience he expresses by repeating his first question in line 2, then asking his rhetorical question, and then, as if he could not leave it, repeating his first question again. We feel him harping on it, dinning it in to the lover. The lover might reply by using the words which Falstaff used to Prince Hal—" O, thou hast damnable iteration, and art, indeed, able to corrupt a saint."

4. The change in rhythm emphasises the change in thought in the poem. The poet is done with his questions and is passing on now to sum up and give you the answer. Thus line 1, stanza 3, begins with two strong accents, " Quit, quit ", which help to convey the peremptory tone. Again, lines 4 and 5 in stanzas 1 and 2 have each three strong accents, but in stanza 3 they have only two strong accents. So the lines seem shorter, as if we were hastening to an evident and satisfactory conclusion. Finally, is there not something satisfactory even in the double rhymes of these lines—" make her " and " take her " ?

The speaker in this poem would have agreed entirely with the speaker of the following lines :

> *Shall I, wasting in despair,*
> *Die because a woman's fair?*
> *Or make pale my cheeks with care*
> *'Cause another's rosy are?*
> *Be she fairer than the day,*
> *Or the flow'ry meads in May,*
> > *If she think not well of me,*
> > *What care I how fair she be?*
> > > *From "The Lover's Resolution" (page 183)*

1. We might compare the extract from " Corinna's going a-Maying " with the poem thus :

      Extract.   Poem.
   Lines 1 and 2. Lines 1 and 2.
     „   3 and 4. Stanza 3.
     „   5 and 6. Stanza 2.
     „   7 and 8. Stanza 4.

Omar Khayyám was a Persian poet and astronomer who lived in the eleventh century. " Fitzgerald's version is rather a new poem inspired by Omar's stanzas than an actual rendering " (Professors Dixon and Grierson).

2. The fourth stanza.
Stanzas 1-3. In these the poet urges us to make the most of our time while we are young, taking as arguments the shortness of the life of flowers, of the course of the sun, and of our own life.
Stanza 4. Here the mood is more peremptory. There are three commands in lines 1 and 2 ; and lines 3 and 4 are also grave.

3. (*a*) Its simplicity and sweetness. See " To the Muses " (page 31) and " To Violets " (page 35).
(*b*) Its directness and frankness. See especially stanza 4.
(*c*) There rings through it that note which has rung through poetry from the earliest times, " In youth is pleasure, in youth is pleasure ", and the regret that youth and beauty fade so fast.

4. Take the fourth stanza :

> *Then be | not coy | but use | your time |*
> *And while | ye may | go mar|ry*
> *For hav|ing lost | but once | your prime |*
> *You may | for ev|er tar|ry.*

In lines 2 and 4 the last foot ends in the middle of the rhyme, there being thus an extra syllable in each line. This applies to lines 2-4 in each of the other stanzas. The extra syllable delays the rhythm and gives it a leisurely effect. In stanza 4, change " marry " to " mate " and " tarry " to " wait " and you will feel the effect of the rhythm :

> *Then be not coy but use your time,*
> *And while ye may, go mate ;*
> *For having lost but once your prime*
> *You may for ever wait.*

I. Sigh no more, Ladies

1. Line 7. The song aims at cheering up the ladies who are sighing at the ways of men. It is as if we said, " Be you blithe and bonny, and don't sigh because men are unfaithful. Men were deceivers ever. They are a bad lot ". But we know that it is not meant, that not all men are deceivers, though some are, that it is merely to cheer the ladies we say they are all alike.

2. I have printed the form I prefer, if for nothing but its appearance on the page. They make two good short rhyming lines, with a natural stop at "so" and they give variety to the rhythm. Printed as one line, however, they give the variety of middle rhyme.

II. O Mistress Mine

3. I think the last two lines :

> *Then come kiss me, sweet-and-twenty !*
> *Youth's a stuff will not endure.*

4. This is happier than the first. It is full of the joy and eagerness of youth.

III. It was a Lover and his Lass

5. (*a*) The original with its varying rhythm, its rhyme, its repetitions is indeed a song, even without music. Read it aloud and you will feel that. By stripping it of its repetitions we have changed the atmosphere, turned it into a rather sober little poem, in rhyming couplets, each couplet a sentence.
(*b*) We have changed the meaning. In each stanza line 3 leads directly into line 4 ; *e.g.* :

> *That o'er the green corn-field did pass, in the spring time, etc.*
>
> *For love is crownéd with the prime, in the spring time, etc.*

IV. Hark ! Hark ! the Lark.

7. Phoebus is the sun and he begins to rise that his steeds may drink the dew that lies on the flowers. Shakespeare has said beautifully what we all know, that the sun dries up the dew.

8. You must choose for yourself.
There are, however, two things to be said for the long line :
(*a*) There is no natural stop at " begin " and in singing we run it on as one long line.
(*b*) " Is " does not rhyme with " begin ". We do not feel this in the long line, but we do in the short line—so much so that " is " becomes " bin " in some versions.

9. The atmosphere of all four is simple and cheerful. II is happier, has more of the joy and eagerness of youth than I. III is the pure gladness of youth, while IV seems to have the very thrill and joy of the lark's song.

1. He tells us each about five times :

Title, .	. Solitary.	Reaper.	
Line 1,	. Single.	In the fields.	
,, 2,	. Solitary.		
,, 3,	. By herself.	Reaping.	Singing.
,, 5,	. Alone.	Cuts and Binds.	
,, 6,	.	..	Sings.
,, 25,	.	..	Sung.
,, 27,	.	..	Work.	Singing.
,, 28,	.	..	O'er the sickle.	
,, 31,	.	..	..	Music.

2. *The Girl*—We know nothing about her except that she is Highland and young.

The Scene—We see a field in a deep Highland valley at harvest time. The road passes close to the field ("Stop here or gently pass") and goes up over the hill. The only descriptive adjective used regarding the scene is " profound ". No adjective of colour is used, but as the girl is reaping we may apply the usual harvest colours.

The Story—There is no story beyond what we have above, that Wordsworth stands listening to the girl and then continues his journey, the music lingering in his memory after he can no longer hear her.

3. From notes 1 and 2 it is evident that these stanzas form only the background for stanzas 2 and 3. As is so often the case, it is not the actual objects or story in which Wordsworth is interested, but the feelings and thoughts they arouse, and these we have in stanzas 2 and 3. Hence we know quite enough about the girl and the scene, and we need no story.

4. You have all heard the statement that familiarity breeds contempt, and you know how quickly scenes and objects lose their first freshness for us. When we come to a beautiful spot, we feel we could be satisfied for ever just to sit and look at it. After we have lived there a week, the spot is still beautiful, of course, but it has lost its first freshness and enchantment. We feel almost that

> *Nothing can bring back the hour*
> *Of splendour in the grass, of glory in the flower.*

But this is just what Wordsworth can do for us. He loves to put before us, not the extraordinary, but the ordinary, and to cast over it that light of freshness and enchantment that makes it strange and new and delightful to us. You have often seen daffodils, but look at them through his eyes and you will see them aglow with happiness,

> *Tossing their heads in sprightly dance.*

But Wordsworth himself had first to see them thus. Something had to awaken the poet in him. Is this not why he says the song is so

welcome ? You will notice that he does not say the song is *beautiful*.
He says it is *welcome*. (In statements like this you can hardly read
Wordsworth too literally.) It comes like the breath of life to the poet
in him, and he thrills to the enchantment of the scene around. For now
he is looking with the eyes of the poet at the wild Highland glen, the
autumn colours, the girl alone in the field, reaping and singing, probably,
an old Gaelic song. What is she singing ? He answers in two of the
finest lines he has written, lines that in their blending of the beautiful
and the strange seem the very essence of romance :

> *For old, unhappy, far-off things,*
> *And battles long ago.*

This is the height to which the song has lifted Wordsworth. Could any
song be more welcome, any experience more thrilling ?

5.   *Breaking the silence of the seas*
           Among the farthest Hebrides.

*   *   *

THE QUEEN OF LOCHLIN (62)

There is no question of our sympathy with the lovers. But we hear
of them only in lines 1-4. The rest deals with the gathering of the
" hardy hosts " and the " mighty stalwarts " and their complete defeat.
In the tale of Troy it is true that we side with the Greeks, but who can
help sympathising with Hector and the Trojans ? And so here, though
we rejoice in the triumph of the lovers, we cannot withhold our sympathy
from the defeated, and probably what will haunt our memory most
will be the great last line :

> *But never one was home returning of all the mighty Lochlin men.*

Compare this last line in its terseness and power with the last two lines
of the following extract from an old Chinese poem (translated by **A.**
Waley) :

> *You served your Prince faithfully,*
> *Though all in vain.*
> *I think of you, faithful soldiers ;*
> *Your service shall not be forgotten.*
> *For in the morning you went out to battle*
> *And at night you did not return.*

*   *   *

THE COUNTRY OF THE CAMISARDS (64)

Take the Japanese poem first. Here the spirit is kindly but sad ; we
feel how futile, how momentary are the ambitions and strife of men.

> *The Worldly Hope men set their Hearts upon*
> *Turns Ashes—or it prospers ; and anon,*
>   *Like Snow upon the Desert's dusty Face,*
> *Lighting a little hour or two—is gone.*

(Omar Khayyám.)

236

Nature neither condemns nor approves this strife. When men die, she receives them back into the earth and grows flowers on their graves. Nature herself might be speaking.

In the passage from " Childe Harold " a man is speaking, and speaking in satire of the littleness of human strife. He makes his contrast bitterly clear, drives his moral home ; but we have not much use for morals in poetry, and though the lines have real power, they lack all sweetness. Compare

How that red rain hath made the harvest grow !

with   *And O, how deep the corn*
          Along the battlefield !

After the harsh bitter strength of Byron's line there is a sweetness in those two lines of Stevenson that is found in the whole poem. For not only was all the land green, but there he found love and peace between the descendants of those who had fought in the country of the Camisards. " And here, after a hundred and seventy years, Protestant is still Protestant, Catholic still Catholic, in mutual toleration and mild amity of life." Even when he speaks of war it is in a kindly way :

They pass and smile, the children of the sword.

The whole spirit of this poem is the triumph of love and peace over fire and war, and of beauty over destruction.

*   *   *

A SONG OF SOLDIERS (65)

1. Probably nothing. Perhaps the frozen dyke and the misty air.
2. Lines 1, 5, 9. He sat musing—day-dreaming.
   Line 3. Marching in the dayshine—the misty air (a far better word here than " daytime ") like a ghost.
   „ 6. Ghostly soldiers.
   „ 7. Marching in the misty air they showed in dreams to me.
   „ 11. Moving like a shadow.

3. When we read the poem, omitting lines 4, 8, and 12, we seem to have robbed it of all sound, so that the soldiers pass before us in the misty air, noiseless, like the army of a dream. You will note they belong to different ages.

4. Line 8 seems full of the noise of the sea—think of the sound of the word "shattering"—yet it is quiet beside line 12. But there is more than the thunder of sound in the last line. It is as if in line 11 the imagination of the dreamer had been fired by the romance of all time, the soldiers moving " to the fate the brave must dree ", and he had cried with Hotspur :

Sound all the lofty instruments of war.
And behind me roared the drums, rang the trumpets of the sea.

1. The contrast will be seen most clearly if we arrange our facts in parallel columns, thus :

Actual Conditions	Dream Conditions
(a) Lack of comfort and freedom. (Perched on his stool at a task.)	Freedom. (Wandering far from all that oppressed him.)
(b) Heat. (Evidently oppressive heat.)	Coolness. (Not cold. The ice, the sea, the drifting snow come as delicious coolness.)
(c) Greyness. (Drab—lack of colour.)	Beauty of colour. (Sapphire blue, emerald green, ruby glow.)
(d) Grime. (Dusty—dirty.)	Cleanness and freshness. (*I'd stripped and I was swimming too* *Through crackling ice and salty deep.* *Snow drifting gently, fine and white.*)
(e) Intolerable street.	Soothing darkness and silence. (*Of everlasting Polar night.*)
(f) Uninteresting work.	Exciting adventure and escape. (*Those big white blundering bulks of death.*)
(g) Struggle to keep awake.	Sleep. (*Sleep drifting deep,* *Deep drifting sleep.*)

2. " Grey," " grimy " ; " blinding ", " blue " ; " thrusting ", " threshing ": " diving ", " doubling ". There are many more

3. You do not feel   *the grey and grimy heat*
         Of that intolerable street
until you wander off with the poet,
        O'er sapphire berg and emerald floe,
and   *Through crackling ice and salty deep,*
and finally nod off to sleep
       Upon that far untravelled shore.
You can actually hear him nodding off to sleep if you read these lines correctly :   *Sleep drifting deep,*
        Deep drifting sleep.
In the same way you do not realise how clean and cool, how restful and peaceful that sleep was, until you suddenly awake to the grimy heat
    Of that intolerable street.

1. One of my students, a beautiful reader, taught this poem before me. Her reading of the poem led me to include it in this anthology.

2. I think it is the frequent use of the four-syllabled foot, and the addition of a syllable at the end of lines 1 and 3 in each stanza.

Take the second stanza :

He could watch them, when he woke, from his window,
With the tall cranes hoisting out the freight,
And he used to think of shipping as a sea-cook,
And sailing to the Golden Gate.

Compare this with the rhythm of " San Stefano " (see Book **III**, page 165).

It was morning at St. Helens in the great and gallant days.

3. (1) Stanza 3. Line 11 sounds dreamy and the lapping of the water is not fast. Line 12 I read thus :

The green and oily water round the keels.

(2) Stanza 8. This is the sad stanza in the poem and goes slowly. Stanza 9. Line 33 I read thus :

He will never never never sail to 'Frisco.

But the pace quickens in the next line and we are back to the old three-beat rhythm, because we are back once more to his day-dreams.

4. No. It is full of the glamour of a boy's dreams. There is one sad stanza, the eighth, but after it we go back to the dreams. He may be a captive, but in his dreams he is free and still finds the old happiness. See " My Lost Youth " (Book III, page 153). Here is one stanza from it :

I remember the black wharves and the slips,
And the sea-tides tossing free ;
And Spanish sailors with bearded lips,
And the beauty and mystery of the ships,
And the magic of the sea.
And the voice of that wayward song
Is singing and saying still :
" A boy's will is the wind's will,
And the thoughts of youth are long, long thoughts."

5 See ' Simon Danz " (page 70)

1. The former poem was full of the unfulfilled day-dreams of a boy, the desire to go out into the world and do something entirely new, such as

Shipping as a sea-cook
And sailing to the Golden Gate.

This one is full of an old sailor's memories of his adventures, of " The great days done ", " The days that are no more ", and ends with the longing to return to the sea and live again some of these great days.

2. Introduction—Stanzas 1-2.

1st picture —   „   3-5.
2nd picture —   „   6-8.
3rd picture —   „   9-11.

See note 5 below.

3. It is for you to say.   But note the differences between them :

(1) This is a picture of contentment, Simon Danz in his Dutch garden dreaming and smiling as he thinks of the things he has accomplished.

(2) Here the past is coming to life, as these old seamen sit

in the shadow and shine
Of the flickering fire of the winter night . . .
While they drink the red wine of Tarragon . .
And they talk of ventures lost and won.

(3) Here the past has come to life and we see Simon Danz pacing his parlour restlessly like a ship riding at anchor (a most appropriate simile) listening to the

Voices mysterious far and near

calling,   " *Come forth and follow me,*"

and feeling,   "*I must down to the seas again*".

Will he go ?

4. Stanza 10, perhaps the best stanza in the poem.   It reminds me of :

Last night a wind from Lammermoor came roaring up the glen
With the tramp of trooping horses and the laugh of reckless men,
And struck a mailed hand on the gate and cried in rebel glee ;
" *Come forth, come forth, my Borderer, and ride the March with me !* "

(See Book III, page 118.)

5. In question 2 you were asked why there was no conclusion.   The answer is that the conclusion is left to you.   Do you see him still riding at anchor though restless at times, or do you see him, like Kipling's voyager

Back once more on the old trail ?

1. (*a*) The house " stands lone " (line 1) and " in the dip of the hill " (line 2). Think how this will seem to cut it off entirely from the rest of the world.
The great owl sits, *i.e.*, is accustomed to sit " over the roof in the branching pine " (lines 3 and 4).
A lonely old man lives there (line 5)

(*b*) The atmosphere of loneliness is necessary if the incident in the poem is to seem real. If it were a busy " cross-roads " and the house the home of a large family, would the story seem as real ? Compare the effect upon you of a ghost story read in the evening when all the family are around, and of the same story read in the same room after all the family have gone to bed.

2. In one sense it is quite true. The old man both hears and sees. He has evidently, in former days, been the toll-gate keeper, when he must often, at night, have heard the sound of galloping horses, have flung open his window with the cry, " Who goes there ? " and then with his lantern gone to open the gate when the traveller has paid the toll. But what he hears and sees *now* you must decide for yourself.

3. It heightens our belief. The old man can see no more, because the traveller (shall we say the phantom traveller ?) rides straight on, " for the toll-gate's gone ". In the old days all travellers had to stop. Now, as the road is free, none stop, not even those who pass on Michaelmas night.

*　　　*　　　*

THE WAY THROUGH THE WOODS (73)

1. We may say that it is definitely suggested three times (lines 1, 5, 12). But in addition we are told :

Line 3.—Weather and rain have undone it again.

Line 6.—Trees have been planted on it.

Lines 7, 8.—Coppice and heath and thin anemones have grown over it.

Lines 10, 11.—The ring-dove broods there, and the badgers (very shy animals) roll at ease.

In fact, the poet devotes the whole stanza to telling us how completely all traces of the old road have been obliterated.

2. See " The Toll-gate House ", note 1 (*b*).
But in telling us that the road is gone, he tells us also how secluded and quiet, how far from the traffic of men it now is, and so prepares us for the next stanza.

3. Stanza 1 has told us so often that there is now no road through the woods
that we should be quite certain of it, but we cannot help wondering why
we are told so often. It almost makes us doubt. It reminds us of the
statement in "Hamlet", "The lady doth protest too much, methinks".
Thus the word "yet" comes as a confirmation of the doubt, and we
wait eagerly to know what is coming.

4. Surely in lines 19-22, where you hear the beat of a horse's feet steadily
cantering through the lines. Note how much more clearly the rhythm
brings out the mid-rhyme in line 19 than in lines 3 and 7. In line 15,
where we cannot miss the mid-rhyme, it is the beauty of sound, "cools",
"pools", that attracts us, just as in line 20 we hear the word "swish",
because the sound so admirably suits the sense.

5. Which is the more convincing you must decide for yourself.
See "The Toll-gate House", note 2 (page 241).
Lines 1-18. These paint beautifully the quietness and seclusion of the
woods. Now note the difference. Drinkwater says the old man both
hears and sees. But Kipling says that if you enter these woods late
of a summer evening you will hear the beat of a horse's feet. And
while we read we hear it in the rhythm. Try to imagine yourself alone
in these woods late on a summer evening, near where the old road used
to run. You would hear many things, and if you say to me that at least
you would not hear what the poem says, I ask you how you can know
until you try.
Do the poems make you for the time being lay aside your ordinary
critical attitude, see and hear with the old man, or hear these riders
" as though *they* perfectly knew the old lost road through the woods " ?
If so, the poems are convincing, and all other questions as to whether they
are true or not are simply absurd and meaningless.

6. See "The Toll-gate House", note 3.
It heightens our belief. It comes as if we were standing listening to the
beat of a horse's feet and the swish of a skirt in the dew, and then
suddenly remembered—but there is no road through the woods.

*　　*　　*

FLANNAN ISLE (74)

1. Yes—the facts of the story are true. Mr. W. W. Gibson, in a lecture
he delivered in Glasgow, said that the story was told to him by the first
man who landed on the island to look for the three who were lost. So
the story comes straight from one of those who

set sail
> *To find out what strange thing might ail*
> *The keepers of the deep-sea light.*

242

Mr. Gibson likes facts, the ordinary facts of life, but his aim is to show us them in a fresh, new light.

It is not difficult to offer an explanation that will fit all the facts of the story. Take this for instance. It is dinner time and one of the three keepers has just finished setting the table and putting the food on it, " meat and cheese and bread ", when he hears a shout from one of his friends. He rushes out, knocking down a chair in his hurry, and leaving the door " ajar ". He finds that one of his friends has fallen into the water and the other is trying to get at him. It is winter. Think of the cold of the water and the waves—even in calm weather you have the long Atlantic swell. Think of the rocky islet and the deep water round it. The attempt at rescue involves the three and they are all swept away. Now, this is all merely imaginary, but surely it is possible enough. Why did some such explanation not suggest itself to the three men who came to seek for " the keepers of the deep-sea light " ?

2. Read lines 89-103. Had you known these facts and had you been one of the three who " set sail " for Flannan Isle, how would you have felt ? It was in this mood they approached the isle. We have a hint of it in lines 7-8. This colours the story from the beginning.

3. Lines 1-88. What seems to me so wonderful about this part of the poem is the manner in which the poet rouses in us the feeling of something strange and horrible without mentioning a single horrible fact. Everything on the island is natural and at peace, but over all hangs this atmosphere of dread. Take for instance lines 13-21. As they approached the island they might naturally expect to get some sign from the keepers, and, getting none, might be worried and anxious, but why should they be

> *struck the while*
> **With wonder all too dread for words** ?

It is their superstitious fear, and does it not explain the next stanza, lines 22-30 ? Does your mind not leap at once to the thought that these " three queer black ugly birds " are the lighthouse keepers ? So we have become superstitious too. Read again lines 1-30 and ask how the poet does it. Is not this Art too ?

4. Yes. Do you not think it one of the finest things in the poem that Mr. Gibson stops where he does ? The first time you read the poem, you expect an explanation, and when none is given you are left wondering. That was the poet's intention. He has shown you the facts in a strange light, so that at the end he leaves you feeling like one of the seekers.

SKATING (78)

This passage was written in Germany, many years after the incidents described.

(*a*) Note how clear and definite the pictures are:

Lines 2-3.   The cottage windows blazed—visible for many a mile.

Lines 10-16.   The game, hare-and-hounds, on the ice.

Lines 20-22.   The stars and the dying sunset.

Lines 24-28.   Chasing the reflection of the star on the polished ice.

Lines 28-29.   The flight before the wind.

(*b*) Lines 5-6.   " For me it was a time of rapture ".   Nothing but deep feeling could have imprinted these pictures so deeply in his memory, not only the sights, but the sounds also.   We hear the village clock strike six, the skates hissing on the ice, the eager voices of the boys and the echoes in the frosty air.   We even " hear " the silence at the close when all was tranquil as a dreamless sleep.

(*c*) He is affected by nature in no ordinary way.

Lines 18-20.   He seems to feel that their wild games disturb the peace of the hills.

Lines 23-24.   Think of him frequently leaving the throng to glide into a silent bay alone, while the rest sweep noisily on.

Lines 24-28.   Again he leaves the throng to chase the reflection of the star.

Lines 28-39.   With a steady wind and plenty of room one can travel thus at fair speed.   But this boy loved to stop suddenly and watch the banks and cliffs apparently go rushing past him.   Spin round rapidly a dozen times and stop suddenly and you see the whole room going round you.   This is the same effect.   He has been gliding rapidly before the wind in the darkness, the banks and cliffs sweeping past.   Think of him stopping suddenly and watching the moving banks and cliffs gradually coming to rest.

If you study these points I think you will feel that he was not an ordinary boy.

*   *   *

THE BOY AND THE OWLS (80)

1. They do resemble each other very closely.   Read again lines 18-39 of " Skating " and you will find that the skater, too, might have blown " mimic hootings to the silent owls ", and probably did.

2. Wordsworth relates this as an experience of the boy of this poem and tells us this boy died when he was twelve.   How then did Wordsworth know ?   He himself had found that at certain moments, when the mind was alert, but not occupied with any particular thoughts, the sights

and sounds of nature would penetrate into his very being. There are certain passages in " Skating ", *e.g.* lines 18-20 and lines 28-39, where we feel he probably has had just this experience. Thus he understood the boy in this poem.

*   *   *

THE HAWK (81)

1. One is inclined to answer " the sunlit air ", **but** there is something before that, the word " slipt ", the effortless glide. Change the hawk to a pigeon and the line becomes ridiculous. The pigeon would " flap ", and noisily, too, out of the pine. Note also the suggestion of ease **in** the words :

   Rose in the unlit air.

   Compare with

   And with strong wings scaling the upward sky,

   describing the flight of the swan (page 20, lines 3-4).

2. " The Buzzards " is a picture of beauty, " The Hawk " a **picture of** beauty and terror, for in it we have the hawk and its prey, the bird. In it also there is a deliberate appeal to pathos—" Oh, would she had dared to rest ! "—suggesting either that the hawk might not have seen her, or refused to strike a motionless prey. But we must not forget the beauty of the hawk, slipping out of the pine, rising, poising, and stooping.

3. This depends on your point of view, whether you feel more the terror and death of the bird (lines 4-8) or the beauty of the hawk (line 1).

*   *   *

THE BUZZARDS (82)

Do you notice that in this poem there is no suggestion that the buzzards ever flap their wings ?
If we are to judge by the frequency with which it is mentioned, next to the flight of the birds, the sunlight is the most important thing in the picture. Take the definite references to **it :**

Line	1.	The warm glow.
,,	6.	The sunny height.
,,	8.	Golden light.
,,	16.	The sunny steep.
,,	19.	Half a mile of sunlight.
,,	25.	Sun-bathed air.
,,	26.	Shining deeps. Fields were golden.
,,	27.	Rosy burned the heather.
,,	30.	Flaming summit.

But the whole poem is bathed in sunlight. **Have we then lost anything** of importance ?

245

We have omitted three passages : (*a*) lines 2-5, (*b*) lines 13-15, and (*c*) lines 20-27.

(*a*) The poem begins with a picture of the beauty of the country in the warm glow, when the sun

> *Through all the long green fields has spread*
> *His first sweet evening yellow.*

It prepares us when we lift our eyes for the picture of the birds in the sunlight, while the homely beauties of the summer evening, the trees and meadows, the cornfields, the reapers and the corn-shocks, by contrast make us feel the height of the birds and the immense sweep of the sky :

> *Serenely far there swam in the sunny height.*

But our feet are still on the earth.

(*b*) Here we are imagining how the birds may feel, how we might feel if we were the birds.

(*c*) Here we are soaring with the birds ; in fact we are the birds and are being " made strong and beautiful in the tide of sun-bathed air ", while far below us, " through shining deeps of air " we see the golden fields and the heather.

Lines 27-29. Once again we are back on earth watching the birds till the sunlight fades from the hill tops.

I think that if you will read now the version on page 83 you will realise that by omitting the three passages we lose the human element in the poem, lose just that which helps us most to live the poet's experience, that which makes the poem a perfect unity.

*   *   *

THE LARK'S SONG (84)

1. Lines 1-10. If we are to appreciate the beauty of the picture in these lines we must try to realise what the street is usually like. For this " A Piper " (Book III, page 65) would help, but perhaps you may find all you need in lines 19-22, which describe the life of the lark in this street. Note the magnificent climax in these lines :

Line 19. The *vile clamour* of the street ;
Line 20. The *insult* of the passing feet ;
Line 21. The *torture* of the daily round ;
Line 22. The organ's *blasphemy* of sound.

Note especially the *insult* (line 20) because he is

> *Bird of the wilderness*
> *Blithesome and cumberless,*

and how could there be human feet passing continuously by his nest ?

Think of his life in these surroundings, his cage, as we learn from another poem in this group, placed " high on the wall ", probably beside some window, two or three storeys up.

2. Lines 1-4. The bird is placed high on the wall above the dull street.
The sunlight slants down and around him. At once the town seems
enchanted, the pinnacles and spires, flashing back the light, seem alive.
Why? Because they are *elate*. This word we use generally only of
persons or living subjects, as, in line 25, " He springs elate ". In line 4,
by giving life to the pinnacle and spire the word emphasises the enchant-
ment worked by the sun.

Compare " Westminster Bridge " (Book III, page 76).

3. Note especially lines 7-9. The one word, " bubbling ", as applied to the
lark's song is an inspiration. In this poem it is the bird's song that
makes more fair

the magic of the sunlit air,

In " The Buzzards " it is the flight of the birds.

4-5. There are twenty-eight lines in this poem. In lines 1-26 we have only
one suggestion of the effect of the lark's song on the people, " above
the *silent* street ", line 5. Why "silent"? But what about line 19, "the
vile clamour of the street"? The lark's song stilled that.

Lines 25-26. Here we feel how hateful the captivity of the bird is to
the poet. Yet he realises that it is only because of its captivity that its
song can come like a blessing to the people in this dull street, giving
to their spirits a few minutes of freedom.

Again the street is grey. What colour had it been while the bird was
singing?

Line 28. *Shut down the windows.* Did you hear the people open them?
Why shut them? There is nothing more worth listening to. They
have been listening, then.

Work-a-day. As the bird is back to its cage

At the rude touch of prison walls,

so they are back to their every-day life. They, too, had attained freedom
in the song of the bird, freedom of spirit but not of body. See " Reverie
of Poor Susan " (Book III, page 75). But all this has been said by the
poet in two lines, a fine example of the power of poetry to say much in
little.

In connection with this poem it would be well to read the little group
of poems including " A Piper ", " The Little Dancers ", " The Contest
in Music ", " Orpheus ", " Reverie of Poor Susan ", " Westminster
Bridge " (Book III, pages 65-76).

1. Line 4. No. Any tree with a good head of foliage would quite change the picture. The poplar, on the other hand, has a long narrow cone of foliage with leaves that tremble in the slightest breeze. Note *shivering* trees, line 10.

2. Line 8. We have but to think of the sunset, then of the pomp of the sunset, and then look for any other adjective to describe pomp, *e.g.*, " wonderful," " glorious," " magnificent," " sublime "—to feel how in strength and dignity both of sound and meaning " incomparable " is by far the best word.
Line 9. There is a chill in the air at sunrise, in this country at least, and a chaste purity about the glories of dawn coming after the darkness of night ; and the word " cold " seems to combine both in one. Note how appropriately we have in the next line " shivering trees ".
Think of the change of atmosphere caused by these four lines, and especially by these two words. In lines 1-6 the tone is bleak, almost sullen, owing to the effect of such words as " naked ", " naked ", " shivering ", " bare ", " bleak ", " bare ". Line 8, with its " incomparable pomp ", lifts us at once into a world of sublime beauty, while line 9 adds a touch of austerity.

3. Line 13. The alliteration is especially effective in the two words so opposite in meaning, " gloom " and " gleam ".

4. Because of the wonderful effects moonlight has on a scene. See " Silver " (Book III, page 114).
Lines 7-10 gave us beauty, sublime and austere.
Lines 13-14 added vivid life.
Line 15 adds a touch of mystery which is strengthened by the " fairy wheel " of line 23 and the " enchant " of line 27.

5. A lonely house on a naked moor. Think of the darkness of the night and the immense sweep of sky, with nothing to dim or interfere with our view of the stars. Even " army " seems hardly sufficient to describe their number.

6. Do you think they are necessary ? Lines 7-30 have shown us so clearly all that these last four lines have to say, that they may seem like a moral tacked on to a beautiful poem. But many admire them. You must decide for yourself.

*   *   *

THE COMMON STREET (88)

1. Line 1. Common.
Line 2. Grey meeting grey. Wearily. To and fro.
Line 3. Patient. Common. (Note it is the common people in the common street.)

Line 4. Sordid burden. Trudging.
Line 5. The rain dropped. (Merely dropped. There is no life or force in it.) See "The House Beautiful" (page 86).
Line 6. Dull, dull, and slow.
Line 8. Faded. Creeping.

I did not realise there were so many till I gathered them together.

2. Line 4. "Sordid" refers not to actual burdens—they would not all be carrying burdens—but to the cares and sorrows weighing on their minds. In lines 9-14, though we are not told it, we feel the glory of the sunset has lifted their minds above them, because it has lifted our minds out of the dull lifelessness of lines 1-8.

3. Gold and black are the two colours suggested in the poem.

4. Line 9. "Burst" gives the feeling of the sudden, unexpected awakening to life. Note "Suddenly" (line 11), "Poured" (line 12). These words emphasise the effect of the word "burst".

5. If the light of the sunset pours down the hill, the hill or street rises towards the West. Think how different the picture would be if it rose towards the North or South, with the houses casting black shadows across it.
Line 13. "A golden highway into golden heaven" would then be absurd.

6. The dark shapes of men would be descending as well as ascending the golden highway, as the people would not all be going the one way. You must decide for yourself whether the poetess was right to leave them out. To me the picture would be beautiful either way.

*   *   *

THE KNIGHT'S TOMB (89)

1. No. There is no suggestion of sadness in this poem, except that which is natural to all life. Death comes in the end, not only to men, but to all living things ; for note (lines 5, 8) even the great oak that lived so long is gone, and the young birch has grown up in its place. You will find this same suggestion of the sadness that is inherent in life in the poem, "To the Virgins, to make much of Time" (page 54).

2. Whenever I begin to read this poem I feel that I want to chant it. There is a good swinging rhythm, and a solemn dignity, especially in the last three lines, that reminds me of a church bell.

3. There is an old-world flavour about this poem. This with the solemn dignity and the rhythm mentioned above gives it the tone of a requiem chanted by the monks.

THE DEAD KNIGHT (90)

1. The last poem was called " The Knight's Tomb ", but there is no suggestion of a tomb or grave here. The knight lay where he fell in some lonely spot on a mountain side. It is a pleasant spot, however, for here we have the clean mountain air, the bees, the grass, the bramble, the harebell, the heather, the vetches, the ivy, the nettle.

2. A " wistful, eerie, thin " note of sadness runs through the poem, due to the pitiful transformation from " the kingly one that his lady loved and his men knew " to a skeleton, but there is so much of the freshness and beauty of the mountain side around, and the poet seems to insist so much upon the peace and restfulness of the scene, that we are at peace, too. Note lines like :

> *The pitiful bones are laid at ease ;*
>
> *Hushed he is with the holy spell ;*
>
> *And he lies quiet and sleeps well ;*
>
> > *The nettle keeps*
> *Vigil about him while he sleeps.*

We are reminded of Shakespeare's lines :

> *Duncan is in his grave.*
> *After life's fitful fever he sleeps well.*

3. We have not here the religious tone of the last poem. There is a definite note of sadness, but also a freshness, a sweetness, a sense of peace and restfulness that lift us above it.

*   *   *

THE TWA CORBIES (91)

1. No. The word "sad" does not describe it at all. It is cynical, harsh like the croak of the raven. At the same time it has the simplicity and clarity of the old ballads.

2. If it were merely gruesome I should object to it, but it is so much more. The cynical note of the third stanza is followed by the great fourth stanza in which the corbies, in language that is almost appallingly clear, seem to me to say with a sort of exultation, " Vanitas Vanitatum— Vanity of vanities, all is vanity ", while the fifth stanza lifts us above human joys and sorrows into the presence of eternity. In the old ballads there is no couple of lines more austere than the last two lines of this poem. What is merely cynical or gruesome could not be poetry. And this *is* poetry, great poetry. But it is so austere and finishes on a note so sublime that it repels some people who miss in it the human note, and see nothing but the gruesome feast of the corbies. The same people dislike the previous poem. They can see in it only the skeleton, and so miss the beauty and peace which surround it.

1. In the last poem we felt especially the lack of the human touch, the not so much inhuman, as non-human, homeless tone.   Here the tone is entirely human, full of a sort of wistful, yearning love.

2. (a) " The Twa Corbies " has no setting.   It stands by itself, alone, creating its own austere atmosphere.
This poem has a setting, one which creates the atmosphere for it.   Read again the conversation between the brothers and you will see how admirably it prepares us for the Song.

(b) " The Twa Corbies " is spoken about the dead knight by one who did not know him and cared nothing for him.
This poem is a personal address to Fidele by those who knew and loved him, expressing an almost passionate desire to console and comfort him.

Note (1) The repetition of the idea : " Fear no more ; all worldly troubles are past."

(2) The absence of any reference to the joys of this world, except

Thou hast finish'd joy and moan.

(3) To die is here spoken of as going home.   How different from the homeless tone of " The Twa Corbies " is the line,

Home art gone, and ta'en thy wages !

(c) " The Twa Corbies " tells a grim story.   In this poem there is no story.   It is a song of farewell.

(d) In " The Twa Corbies " the language is bare, bald, austere.   In this poem the language reflects the characters of the speakers.   They are simple and direct, warm-hearted and sincere, with a natural dignity and restraint, due to their birth and their upbringing.   Apply these adjectives to the poem, *e.g.,*

Simple and Direct.	*Thou thy worldly task hast done, Home art gone and ta'en thy wages. To thee the reed is as the oak, Thou hast finish'd joy and moan.*
Warm-hearted and Sincere.	*Golden lads and girls.* It is only when we try to substitute some word for " golden " that we realise what a wonderful adjective it is, how it sums up the warmth, the joy, the sunshine of youth. *All lovers young, all lovers must.* The repetition here seems to say, " Young lovers, even as young as you, must come to this."
Dignity and Restraint.	Do you not feel as if the lamentation ended at line 18 ? In lines 19-24 they are bidding the final farewell. Note how the change in rhythm helps this ; lines 19-22 have only three strong beats each, the shortness of the line helping to emphasise the restraint.

The song, " Hark, Hark, the Lark " (page 58), was also sung to Imogen
(Fidele) in the earlier part of this play.

*   *   *

DEATH THE LEVELLER (95)

1. In a way they would, but we should miss the emphasis. All must come
down to dust would be nearer it. The burden of this poem is that the
mighty ones of the earth must all come down in death to the level of
common men. Shirley expresses the same idea in " The Last Conqueror ":

> *Victorious men of earth, no more*
> > *Proclaim how wide your empires are ;*
> *Though you bind-in every shore,*
> *And your triumphs reach as far*
> > *As night or day,*
> *Yet you, proud monarchs, must obey*
> *And mingle with forgotten ashes, when*
> *Death calls ye to the crowd of common men.*

In addition, the sentence quoted omits the fine reference to the actions
of the just (lines 23 and 24) which alone death cannot touch.

2. I should choose lines 5-8, and 23-24.

3. The last poem was wistful, loving, full of the sadness of a personal loss.
There is no sadness here. This is the voice, rather cold and hard, of a
stern preacher, telling of the vanity of human glory, but ending on a
note of high religious fervour.

4. The change in atmosphere is due to the following :

(*a*) The absence of the personal note. This poem is a warning to all
men of all times.

(*b*) The personification of Death—see especially the splendid line,
" Death lays his icy hand on kings "—and the highly metaphorical
language used. In this it forms a fine contrast to the language of the
preceding poem (see note 2 (*d*) page 251). The only line in it which
resembles the language of " Death the Leveller " is line 11 :

> *The sceptre, learning, physic, must*
> *All follow this, and come to dust.*

(*c*) The moral tone, especially in the last two great lines :

> *Only the actions of the just*
> *Smell sweet, and blossom in their dust.*

*   *   *

OZYMANDIAS (96)

1. The entire absence of the didactic or teaching tone. Fine as the pre-
ceding poem is, it does preach at us a little. Shirley has a moral to
impress and he does it splendidly. But that is not the business of
poetry. In " Ozymandias " you see the true way of poetry. Shelley

paints the scene so vividly that in imagination we are there ; we see the shattered visage, read the words on the pedestal, look around—and that is all. If you have felt and seen, you have understood. Similarly in " Fear no more the Heat o' the Sun " there is nothing taught, there is no kind of moral or lesson. But when we read the poem we see the scene, become one of the mourners, feel at once the personal loss, the wistful yearning love for the " golden lad " that lies apparently dead. And that is poetry.

2. Lines 4-8 and 10-11. But surely more significant than these is the fact that Ozymandias must have commanded the statue to be built, and the words to be put on the pedestal.

3. If there is any doubt about the meaning of this sentence, the general analysis may make it clear. In this way, occasionally, grammar can help us in interpreting a poem.

4. The hand is evidently the hand of the sculptor. That he was a real artist is proved by lines 6-7. What has the sculptor done ? He has made live what should have died, the sneer of cold command, the pride and arrogance of Ozymandias, and we look round on the lone bare desert and feel how small indeed were Ozymandias and his power. Is this not mockery ?

5. Think of the words on the pedestal and note how the answer, which is apparently complete in the three words, " Nothing beside remains ", seems to grow in volume and width of meaning, as if the infinite were replying to the finite.
Note the cumulative effect of such words as,
Line 12. " decay ",
Line 13. " wreck ", " boundless and bare ",
Line 14. " lone and level ", " stretch far away ".

*　　*　　*

EGYPT'S MIGHT IS TUMBLED DOWN (97)

1. We have lost (a) the rhythm, (b) the effect of the sound of the repetition of " down ", and (c) the emphasis.
What we are apt to forget is that these are all part of the meaning. Mr. de la Mare has said that the meaning of a line of poetry is the whole effect it has on us. Hence rhythm and sound are part of the meaning, and you cannot give the meaning of the two lines except by quoting them. If you change a word, or omit one, or change the order of the words, it may make little difference to you, but a poet is always far more keenly interested in the exact meaning and significance and sound of words than we are, far more sensitive to their effects. So when he has said a thing—well, that is what he means. In fact, he says what he means and means what he says. (See Practice in Rhythm, note 2, page 209, and Practice in Rhyme, note 1, page 212.)

255

2. It is nearly two thousand years since the birth of Christ. We are told that the Egyptians were a civilised people more than four thousand years before the birth of Christ. Try to think back four, five, or six thousand years, and you seem to go down to the deeps of thought.

3. (a) " We are the Music-makers " (page 21).
   (b) See note 2, page 215.

4. We might think that we had gained two things :
   (a) Emphasis—This is the most common effect of introducing " alone ", *e.g.*, " He alone offered ".
   (b) By introducing this word we have made line 10 similar in rhythm to line 5, a thing we should probably expect.

In reality, however, we have lost the real emphasis which the poet gives to line 10, a far more arresting emphasis, due to the break in the rhythm. We expect a line of three beats and are brought up short by the fact that there are only two. Think of a company of soldiers marching, the regular rhythm of left-right, left-right, and then, the effect of the command, " Halt ! " The break in the rhythm draws us up as it does the company of soldiers. This is the effect produced in line 10, and it gives splendid emphasis to the words.

5. The dream of Ozymandias has " tumbled down " with Egypt's might. He was not one of the " music-makers " or " dreamers of dreams ". He was not a " world-loser " or a " world-forsaker ". The Bible says, " He that loseth his life shall find it." We might say, " He that gaineth this world shall lose it." Ozymandias, King of Kings, dreamt only of his own greatness. No truly great man thinks himself great.

* * *

WHERE ROSE THE MOUNTAINS (98)

1. Shelley says of Byron, " He is a person of the most consummate genius. . . . But it is his weakness to be proud : he derives from a comparison of his own extraordinary mind with the dwarfish intellects that surround him, an intense apprehension of the nothingness of human life. His passions and his powers are incomparably greater than those of other men."

You will, I think, feel in these two stanzas his genius and his incomparable passion and power, and in the second stanza the effect of his pride. You have seen them in " The Shipwreck " from " Don Juan " (Book III, page 61). You will see them again in this book.

2. To me the most expressive word is " but ". After the glories of the first stanza it comes like a fatal warning of the change. You have only to try any other conjunction in its place, such as " and ", " however ", " though ", to feel how much we need the word " but ".

3. To me the picture is in stanza 2, lines 3-4, while the line,

> *To whom the boundless air alone were home,*

is one of the most powerful Byron has written.

4. The pride of Ozymandias is that of the little mind of the tyrant king who glories in his own apparent greatness. Byron's pride is that of the great mind which finds its home among the great things of the world and cannot brook the restrictions of the apparent littleness of human life, even in himself. He expresses the idea in an earlier stanza (III, 6) in the words :

> *What am I ? Nothing : but not so art thou,*
> *Soul of my thought.*

*   *   *

THE OCEAN (99)

1. Compare the two stanzas carefully and you will find they are different expressions of thoughts rising practically from the same feelings. Read again Turgenev's description of the seagull (page 22) and ask yourself if it does not seem to you to symbolise the spirit of Byron.

2. In an earlier stanza (III, 90) he expresses the same feeling thus :

> *Then stirs the feeling infinite, so felt*
> *In solitude, where we are least alone.*

Matthew Arnold puts it :

> *" Ah, once more," I cried, " ye stars, ye waters,*
> *On my heart your mighty charm renew ;*
> *Still, still let me, as I gaze upon you*
> *Feel my soul becoming vast like you."*

3. The littleness of man and all his works in comparison with the sea.

4. " Lay " is substituted for " lie "—for the sake of the rhyme. This is a common English provincialism, but quite indefensible here.

5. (a) That, while everything else changes, the sea remains " unchangeable "

   (b) *Time writes no wrinkle on thine azure brow—*
   Such as creation's dawn beheld, thou rollest now.

6. This stanza agrees well with the fact that

> *Egypt's might is tumbled down.*

It has not, however, the same hope for man as we find in the lines,

> *But the dreams their children dreamed . . .*
> *These remain.*

7. That the Ocean is alone worthy to be the mirror of the Almighty,

> *The image of Eternity, the throne*
> *Of the Invisible.*

In fact, that it is " boundless, endless, and sublime ".

8. In stanzas 2-4 Byron is trying to make us realise the littleness of man and his works, and our minds are fixed on that. In 5-6 he is trying to make us feel the greatness, the sublimity of the changeless sea.

9. No. Byron is rightly finishing on the note of love, and so here we forget the sublimity of the sea which fills us with awe, and think of the charm it has for us, which makes us love it. In an earlier stanza (III, 2) Byron addresses the sea thus:

> *Once more upon the waters! Yet once more!*
> *And the waves bound beneath me as a   steed*
> *That knows his rider. Welcome to their roar!*

*   *   *

TO GREECE (102)

1. It is interesting to note that a Greek poet living some five hundred years B.C., the famous Simonides of Ceos, in an epigram on the men who had fallen in the Persian Wars, said, " These being dead yet live ", and Byron 2300 years later calls them "the unforgotten brave".

Thermopylae. In this famous pass Leonidas and the Spartans held up the advance of the whole Persian Army. When warned that the enemy were sending a large body of men over the hills to attack them in the rear, they refused to retreat, and fought till every man was slain.

In " The Charge of the Light Brigade " Tennyson says:

> *Their's not to make reply,*
> *Their's not to reason why,*
> *Their's but to do and die:*

This was entirely the position of the Spartan soldier; and Simonides in the epitaph he wrote on the men who fell at Thermopylae, suggests it. " Stranger, bear word to the Spartans that we lie here obedient to their charge."

Salamis, the scene of the great naval victory of the Greeks over the Persians. The battle meant to the Greeks what the defeat of the Armada meant to Elizabethan England.

2. A grave is a place where a person is buried and, in time, forgotten; a shrine, a place where he is worshipped and remembered.

3. We feel the passion and the power in the very first line and they swell and rise to the great climax in lines 21-23. These three lines are among the greatest Byron has written, among the greatest things that have ever been said of liberty.

4. We have alternate rhyme, rhyming couplets, and rhyming triplets. It is in the triplets that we find both the weakness and the strength. Byron uses the rhyme to mark and bind together the thought, as in lines 10-11, 12-13. But in the triplets, lines 14, 15, 16, the first two lines express one thought, while the third begins a new one which is completed in a different rhyme. We feel, therefore, that the structure somewhat weak and unfinished. On the other hand the rhyme in 21-23—" begun ", " son ", " won "—strengthens and binds ly together the thought of this wonderful triplet.

2. You will notice I asked which point of view, not which poet, appeals to you, for we cannot judge a poet by one poem or extract. For instance, Wordsworth loves the mountains at least as much as Byron, and Byron loves freedom at least as much as Wordsworth. You must decide for yourself which point of view appeals more to you, but try to see both clearly before you decide. Byron's is personal, the passionate feeling of a strong man, strongly expressed. Hence he tends to carry us entirely with him. Wordsworth's is almost impersonal, as if he spoke not for himself but for everyone. It is less passionate but has wonderful dignity and strength. Think, for instance, of the picture in the line

Where not a torrent murmurs heard by thee.

3. See note 2. No. In Wordsworth's poems you rarely find passion. The poem is called " *Thought* of a Briton ". Wordsworth held that poetry should spring from " emotion recollected in tranquillity ". Poetry so written will show less evidence of passion than Byron's, which was written in a white heat of feeling, but will probably have more depth and dignity.

4. The poem is a prayer to the spirit of Liberty. Any name suggesting that would be suitable.

5. Note the name of the poem, " Thought of a Briton " and remember that Napoleon was threatening the liberty of Britain. At that time Britain was regarded as the ruler of the sea. Hence the conquest of Britain would mean the conquest of the sea. The whole poem is an expression of his love of his own land.

*　　　*　　　*

BREATHES THERE THE MAN (104)

1. You will notice that the language is simpler, less figurative, more direct than that of the other two poems. At the same time there is strong feeling in it strongly expressed. From this poem, then, we should think him a devoted lover of his country ; and in speech, strong, simple, and direct.

2. In his love of his country he resembles Wordsworth, but in style he resembles Byron. In this poem he is less passionate and powerful than Byron, but more direct, and, in the second stanza, more personal.

3. The Englishman would choose lines 1-3 ; the Scotsman, I think,

Land of brown heath and shaggy wood,
Land of the mountain and the flood.

1. From the Parable of the Good Samaritan (Luke x. 30-37).

2. Before you answer the question read again stanzas 4-9. In these six stanzas we are told that the man is sitting dreaming of his past life, and we have five perfect little pictures of his boyhood, his school and university life, and his voyage out to India. These tell us clearly the character of the man, but what have they to do with the story ? The poem consists of twelve stanzas, and here we seem to have disposed of six. But the question goes deeper than that. Read again stanza 2. Surely that is telling the story ! Well, but is it not just as clearly describing the character of the man ? Why, the first two words of the stanza, " He laughed ", tell us a fact in the story, it is true, but we feel at once that only one kind of man would laugh under these circumstances. Why are we so interested in the story ? Because of the greatness of the character of the man. And so stanzas 4-9, even if they seem not to be part of the story but a revelation of his character, are of vital importance to the story because they have so deepened our interest in the man. This is the way in every good story. Each incident throws light on the character and the character gives life and meaning to the incident. If you were told that the man in this story was really a coward or a miser, you would at once say the story was impossible. But because of the character of the man we feel the story true, that, in the words of Napier, " for such a man Death is not a Leveller ".

3. (*a* and *b*) If you have understood note 2, above, then you know at once that this is not a sad poem, because of the character of the man which makes the story live. Surely the effect is not one of sadness. It lifts and inspires us. We might say in Milton's words :

> *Nothing is here for tears, nothing to wail*
> *Or knock the breast, no weakness, no contempt,*
> *Dispraise, or blame, nothing but well and fair,*
> *And what may quiet us in a death so noble.*

And so if we changed " slept " to " wept ", we should finish on quite a wrong note.
It is as if Newbolt said to us—It is not death that matters, but life, and so long as we are living a full, true life, not merely existing, but living to the full power of our being, then we are ready at any moment to pass through the gate of death into the great beyond. The poet, however, has done far more than merely say that. He has made us live with the man and die with him, and so we are convinced. We know, we feel that it is true.

2. We might say that in stanza 1 they are marching up into position, in stanza 2 working up closer to the enemy, preparatory to the attack, and in stanza 3 making the final desperate charge. Note here the effect of the alliteration in " rising, roaring, rushing ", and how finely the sound suits the sense in the two words " roaring, rushing ".

3. It seems to be Newbolt's practice to state the bald fact of death as plainly and simply as possible :

A sword swept (page 106)

Thirty bullets straight where the rest went wide,
And thirty lads are lying on the bare hillside.

Thus in neither poem is there any attempt to soften or hide the fact. But in each the lines that follow somehow make death look cheap We feel that here is character and courage to which death comes but as the gate to the great adventure beyond. See " Admiral Death ", note 1.

* * *

ADMIRAL DEATH (110)

1. Here again as in the last two poems we have the same bald statement of the fact of death :

Their bones are white by many a shore,

while in the last four lines death is spoken of as if he were one of the Valkyries. Those spirits rode over the heads of the warriors in the battle and picked out the bravest, who died at once and were carried off to eternal happiness in Valhalla.

Oh ! but they loved him, young and old,
For he left the laggard, and took the bold.

2. Yes, I think it makes clearer than either of the others how we are to regard death. Take the references to him.
Stanza 1. He is the chief admiral of the fleet.
Stanza 2. We have the rules of his service.
Stanza 3. We see his love for the brave, for they are to know him
By the tenderest eyes of all that are.
Stanza 4. We see how the brave love him.
He is regarded as a god. His reward for some of the brave is that they shall die in the fullness of their life and strength.

They shall grow not old, as we that are left grow old:
Age shall not weary them, nor the years condemn.

INDEX OF FIRST LINES